REINVENTING SIERRA LEONE

Literary and Post-Conflict Essays

Gbanabom Hallowell

Philadelphia

Re-inventing Sierra Leone
Literary and Post-Conflict Essays

Copyright © 2020 Gbanabom Hallowell.
All rights reserved. No part of this book may be used or reproduced by any means, graphic, electronic, or mechanical, including photocopying, recording, taping or by any information storage retrieval system without the written permission of the publisher except in the case of brief quotations embodied in critical articles and reviews.

Africanist Press books may be ordered through booksellers or by contacting:
Africanist Press
5114 Race Street
Philadelphia, PA 19139
www.africanistpress.com

+1-347-569-1978 (United States)
Email: africanists@yahoo.com • africanistpress100@gmail.com

Because of the dynamic nature of the Internet, any web addresses or links contained in this book may have changed since publication and may no longer be valid. The views expressed in this work are solely those of the author and do not necessarily reflect the views of the publisher, and the publisher hereby disclaims any responsibility for them.
Any people depicted in stock imagery provided by Thinkstock are models, and such images are being used for illustrative purposes only.Certain stock imagery © Thinkstock.

ISBN 978-0-9969739-0-8

Printed in the United States of America.

"We are constantly reinventing our traditions in the various stories we tell ourselves about ourselves, incorporating new experiences and material"
- *Cambridge English Corpus*

For my teachers and my students
who patiently taught me
how to read and how to write

Contents

ON LITERARY ARTS

1. A Re-examination of Face 9
2. Manufacturing Mocking Stones 33
3. African Verse and the Cultural Forces of World Poetry 45
4. Scarification and Memory 63
5. Pictures of Shame 67
6. A Fireside of Poems and Chants 75

ON CULTURAL VALUES

7. Feeding, Eating and the Politics of Food 91
8. Upholding Ethical Values as Corruption Prevention Measure ... 101
9. A Taste of Nationhood 111
10 Toward a Creative Liberal Education 115
11. Theorizing African Narrative Mediation 129
12. Reading the Political Resume of a War Time Leader 147

ON THE MEDIA

13. The Need to Improve the Media in West Africa 165
14. Addressing Human Rights in the Sierra Leone Media 171
15. The Seismic Shift in the Media Landscape 187

PART ONE
ON LITERARY ARTS

CHAPTER 1

A Re-examination of Face

Falui Poetry Society (FPS), resilience and the poetic trajectory of Sierra Leone's dirty war and *Blood Diamond*s.

In 1991, Sierra Leone's infamous civil war broke out. Two years earlier, an African American Professor, Fred Woodard of the University of Iowa had come to Sierra Leone on a cultural exchange of ideas to discuss the general studies of American short stories, a program sponsored by the American Embassy in Freetown, Sierra Leone. The war had barely begun. Shortly after the brief visit of Professor Woodard, the Falui Poetry Society (FPS) the only such known interwar literary, specifically, poetry group in Sierra Leone was formed.

It was a period of disillusionment. While all around creative writing was flourishing, Sierra Leone literally remained unproductive. The love for the arts and the resilience with which the budding poets kept going retreat after retreat was startling, to say the least. It was like an unending academy of fine arts in a writing class, only it didn't receive a university testimonial.

The war had been raging, and suddenly the poets discovered

a way of converting their retreats into a court of conscience to write and critique each other's poems, mostly and thematically on their conducts. Not that the poets had any office of political authority to influence the cause of the war; however, exciting creative pieces of exercises in terms of writing resulted in panels of assessments as it were.

While the pain, trauma, and the deaths were occurring, the international community added to the shock of a scandal that the Sierra Leonean and Liberian wars had been discovered to be characterized by dirty deals of blood diamonds. Throughout the scandal, FPS was heavy-ladened, but the members pressed on with determination to change the trajectory on the page. With this thought in mind, my paper follows the historical events until the success of the publication of an anthology, *Songs That Pour the Heart*, becoming the first anthology of war poems since the end of the war. The book contains 121 poems written by 18 poets over a period of eight years.

Wars in the Minds of Men

U Thant is known for saying that, "Wars begin in the minds of men." The Sierra Leonean war of the 1990s that lasted a decade was not only atrocious but also dirty and illicit in transaction. By the middle of the war, the enterprise was too expensive to prosecute both for those who fashioned the war and those who prosecuted it. No sooner had the war began than it became geographically challenging and costly to manage in terms of the behavioral discipline of the mercenaries and the focus of the organization's toxic leadership.

The two countries of Sierra Leone and Liberia, which jointly contributed to the private manpower for the mercenary engagement of events, perpetrated dastardly mayhem. A postulation of the next phase would have seen the crude liberation of cronies under the dictatorship in a Utopian unification of the two countries. We have to consider that it was a design that Muammar Gaddafi, the godfather had calculated for the two wars, to benefit from his idealistic leadership style as were most of the projects he envisioned in Libya or those of wider Africa where he touted the idea of a confederation of African states. Smillie (2010) noted, that the notorious warlord, "Taylor backed Sankoh's fledgling Revolutionary United Front, giving it a Liberian base, weapons, and an outlet for whatever it could steal in Sierra Leone." Much of the success of that transaction was the cross border camaraderie between the two countries.

The planners of the war were not only friends but also, in many instances, blood relatives from across each other's border. Smillie added that "After a stint in Benghazi learning the arts of revolutionary warfare from teachers assigned by Muammar Gaddafi, Sankoh created the Revolutionary United Front (RUF)." For a better understanding of the literary histrionics, read Hallowell's novel, *The Road to Kaibara*.

During that period when the war became a purely Sierra Leonean affair, in their little corner, a small group of poets, the Falui Poetry Society (FPS), was engaged in a court of conscience and was prosecuting on a daily basis the conduct of the war. Although the two countries of Sierra Leone and Liberia were, no doubt, equally engaged in the poetry of each other's countries, no evidence existed that bilateral readings, performances, or festivals occurred during or after the war. Obviously, it would have been practically impossible to communicate, especially then, when there was no technology of social media.

The status of Creative Writing in Sierra Leone before the War

A few years ago, I published an anthology of short stories called *In the Belly of the Lion*. The brief introduction I wrote suffices to a word or two on the literary tradition of Sierra Leone. Sierra Leone grew up to become a West African nation constituted as a unitary state under a deliberate Athenian value system that, ironically, initially deprived the country from breeding citizens interested in developing their own local literary tradition, as it was for a long time intoxicated in a truly European Pierian Spring. The British literary tradition and all its contextual foxtrots lulled the country into comfortably assimilating the colonizer's literary archival treasures. It converted the poor nation into suffocated Anglo-Saxons and dutiful servants to the daiquiri of western cannons that had well become indisputably universal in a truly colonial sense of the expression.

It is important to say a word or two about the link between the country's contemporary writers and their past counterparts, if only because we must develop a sense of the connection that demonstrates a continuum in the emergence of the country's literary tradition. How much inspiration did the current generation of writers derive from the past generations? How have the works of the past influenced the works of the current generation of writers? How much mentorship did the past generation provide for the succeeding generation of writers? Much of what came out as creative writing by Sierra Leonean writers of the colonial and immediate post-colonial period emerged from the capital city of Freetown. Other regions recorded almost nothing, despite the fact that, in oral form, local folklores and social stories flowed like a river around bonfires and other gatherings.

Meanwhile, in Freetown, exciting materials were being produced largely in the genre of drama, mostly for the pleasures of the lingering colonial masters and the growing krio intelligentsias. In the initial period, these dramas were mostly caricatures of works by Shakespeare and other British writers localised in language and in colour. Important local talents, such as Thomas Decker, who wanted to tell their own stories their own way, began surfacing, even stronger in their ability to represent their own culture and tradition more successfully than they had represented the true aura of the British theatre.

Thomas Decker's generation was to serve as an inspiration for writers of the succeeding generations; however, this scenario was not always true for writers of fiction and poetry. For those areas, future writers mostly looked up to the then-growing crops of neighbouring Nigerian and Ghanaian writers. To make matters worse for the future, Sierra Leonean writers, their school syllabi were heavily loaded with Nigerian and Ghanaian writers, such as Chinua Achebe, Wole Soyinka, Ayi Kwei Armah, and Ama Ata Aidoo.

It was not that there were no Sierra Leonean novelists and poets at the time. A few, such as Wellesly Cole, Abioseh Nicol, Sarif Easmon, and Delphi King, were themselves entering the international circles, albeit, lethargically. The reality was that the majority of the Sierra Leonean writers then either treated their writings as deeply personal affairs, thereby availing them to little avenues of publishing, or they were writing in exile.

I have mentioned elsewhere that the erudite Sierra Leonean scholar, Eldred Durosimi Jones, had shared with me that the Sierra Leonean was mostly a conformist as opposed to being truly creative. Such posture had accounted for the dearth in materials that came out in the way of creative writing in the early hours of independent rule compared to the high percentage of citizens who benefited from early western education to the envy of other West African countries.

By the time the war started, writers had become a rare species among Sierra Leoneans. The theatre, which had accounted for the highest form of creative writing, had been mutilated by an uncompromising political atmosphere. Lone voices, such as those of Syl Cheney-Coker, Dele Charley, Muctarr Mustapha, and Amadu (Yulisa) Pat Maddy, could either produce in exile or write only for the audience of their cupboards. Thus, the two decades of the 1970s and 1980s wasted without any meaningful literary river flowing in country!

The 1990s exhibited the hangover effect of the malaise of the strangulation of the country's creative voice and of the educational system in the 70s and 80s. No longer was any Sierra Leonean comfortable to tout about Sierra Leone being the "Athens of West Africa." History had betrayed the country, and her daughters and sons did not feel that they had any evidence in terms of production to show that the country was the doorway for education in the sub region. However, as evil and devastating the war was, it brought about a re-emergence of defiance and a literary plenipotentiary in the many that wanted to speak truth to power! Soon pockets of literary groups began meeting to inspire each other.

Founding of Falui Poetry Society (FPS)

By the middle of the war when the Economic Community of West African States (ECOWAS) under the leadership of Nigeria had invaded the mercenaries of both Liberia and Sierra Leone in a bilateral show of support to the governments of both Liberia and Sierra Leone, it became difficult for the private and illegal armies to fraternize in combat on each other's borders. Subversively, however, to thwart the effort of ECOWAS intervention, the traffic of communication of personnel and warfare among the illegal forces of Liberia, Sierra Leonean and Libyan network of godfathers posed many problems in time, yet, the multilateral force remained committed to frustrate the mercenary organization. In spite of the upper hand and arrangements on the side of the multidisciplinary force, the war raged longer and more vigorously.

The question then becomes, is it not conclusive that any violent exchange with a maximum scale casualty of death is dirty? Are all wars dirty? Ethically speaking, wars of liberation or those that see a people standing up for themselves are often clean wars. As in the case of this article, wars are usually dirty when they are initiated unjustly and are administered under corrupt circumstances. In the war under consideration it became clear that it was dealt with a heavy blow of corruption. Lans Gberie's *A Dirty War in West Africa: RUF and the Destruction of Sierra Leone* is a compelling and compassionate account of the atrocities suffered particularly by the vulnerable lot of children and women.

As I had stated earlier, the African American, Professor Fred Woodard had arrived at a dramatic period. The war had barely begun. Shortly after the brief visit of Professor Woodard, the FPS was formed. By this time, the war was enough to attract national issues, and Falui was focused on responding to the bad rumors of the vivid destruction of life and property. Hardly anyone among us in the group was strategic enough to influence the cause of the war, but the weekly gathering had writers with the strongest of opinions and creative writing was an outlet.

In 2004, four years after the nation declared the end of the war, the poets who had followed throughout with their resilience, contributed their own money and paid for the production of an anthology, appropriately called *Songs That Pour the Heart*. With the commitment to stick together since the founding, the courageous followership of being children of their own country, Sierra Leone, the group endured. In the 'outdooring' of the book, one of the members, Mohamed Gibril Sesay, who wrote the foreword, unfolded perhaps the country's successful resilience in literary history in Sierra Leone. He wrote:

> We have come a long way with these songs. They pour the heart because we feel that hearts are what are needed to irrigate/reclaim our societies in a fashion nourishing enough for the humane growth of whosoever reads or listen to them. Sad recounting tinged with hopes of fertile times, eclectic narratives mirroring the rainbow influences on our experiences; our songs are also memories of moments during the decade of deluge. They are paeans of fortitude, hope and faith; they are dreams of the rainbow happening that would end the deluge and restore the land.

There are many reasons to be proud of the publication of that anthology. Eighteen years after 1993 when the FPS was founded, producing a copy of that nature and gathering eighteen poets to contribute to the anthology was a dream project. It took those eighteen poets a combination of war years to accomplish the production of the anthology. Never again would such a literary history be made in Sierra Leone as was made by those eighteen poets in all those years.

For the poets who cherish this history, two anniversaries have become important in the literary history of Sierra Leone. Twenty-six years ago, the FPS was founded in 1993, and fifteen years ago, in 2004, the iconic anthology, *Songs That Pour the Heart* was published. The then-president of FPS, Rev. Moses Kainwo, who wrote the afterword when the anthology was published didn't hide his society's accomplishment:

> There have been trail blazers in this art in Sierra Leone long before some of us were born. We shall endeavor to feature them in subsequent editions. We are also aware that some people have kept their writings in cupboards because they have not got the means to publish them. Indeed we now have well-meaning Sierra Leoneans ready to promote the publication of good literature. So with pen and paper around, what stops us from writing?

It was such an emotional account, of publishing, and even more a resilience of hope. One could see the excitement as the promise of subsequent anthologies and editions were imagined in the future libraries and bookshops. That was years ago when manuscripts were done by hand and had to be stored times over from one cupboard to another and at the mercy of rats not chewing sentences and phrases away until a publishing opportunity came around. It is the altruism that is instantly shared with would-be writers that characterized the success of the group.

Since the publication of the anthology, no other anthology has been published in the name of the society; however, it is suffice to say that a single-most feat had been accomplished. Some of the eighteen poets who are in the anthology have gone on to write collections of their own poems. Maybe to mark the fifteenth anniversary of the anthology, it would be good to republish the anthology, but much effort would be needed to ensure that its content is not changed.

The account went on to state that when the anthology was published, the vice president of the country, Solomon Berewa, graced the occasion. At once, it was a truth proved that art had stood tall! From its humble beginning, art was being recognized.

Following the war, the world had supported the government to set up the Special Court of Sierra Leone. When the anthology was published, the chief prosecutor who had attended the launching ceremony took a copy of the book overnight. On the day he was to address the court, without any prompt, he took out a copy of the anthology. Oumar Farouk Sesay documented the happenings of the court room and he wrote:

> The chief prosecutor, David Crane, stood up to give his opening statement. He started by cataloguing the inhumanity to a courtroom packed full with the world media, there was a deafening silence. He removed the book, Songs That Pour the Heart, containing poems of members of Falui Poetry Society. He read a poem written by Sydnella Shooter, a female teacher and founding member of the Society. Symbolically, a poet became the first witness called in a trial meant to stop the cycle of impunity. The somber mood in the courtroom climaxed when the lines dripped like a torrent of bullets.

If poetry was meant to be recited as Homer and all his courtiers had intended it, if the African traditional chiefs with all their ensembles, and if a gathering where men and women were held accountable for the actions of a dirty war of blood diamonds, then FPS had arrived, seen and conquered. How sad the country didn't capture that moment, uphold what Oumar Farouk Sesay described as "somber mood."

Giusti has noted that "The crystallized moment—which encapsulates situation—moves toward the final sigh that is the threshold to the fullness of experience and from where the poem can begin (again)."

Fast forward, Falui continues to linger with age, still not sure to reawaken from slumber or relegate to the museum of literary history, for it is important, for posterity and for the founding members, numbering not more than ten, Ousman Barrie,

Gbanabom Hallowell, Moses Kainwo, Ambrose Massaquoi, Musu Sandy, Mohamed Gibril Sesay, Oumarr Farouk Sesay, Sydnella Shooter, James Taylor, Tatafway Mani Tumoe, before being joined at different later periods by Bridget Olamide James, Frederick Borbor James, Wiltshire Johnson, Daphne Kaikai, Jonathan Kpakiwa, Nathaniel Pearce, Daphne Pratt and Kosonike Koso-Thomas.

The Dirty Face of the Sierra Leone War

Although hundreds of research engines described dirty wars, not one could satisfactorily define the term, "dirty war." Dictionary.com defines it as "a war conducted by the military or secret police of a regime against revolutionary and terrorist insurgents and marked by the regime's use of kidnapping, torture, and murder, with members of the civilian population often the victims." For the purpose of my paper, I have attempted a definition that a dirty war is the subterfuge that characterizes the engagement of war in which the authorities involved convert into a rogue power force to subvert the masses of civilians and military and goodwill ambassadors, resulting in physical and psychological consequences on the character of the nation.

What distinguishes between the earlier definition from my own definition is that mine explores the character of dirty ploys, trickery, and of deception whereas the first definition has no reference of foil and treachery. As it will be demonstrated, Sierra Leonean poets of the war generation captured the trickery and deception that were responsible for casualties of vulnerable civilians and courageous military fighters who perished senselessly. There was a time when deception was a bait to lure civilians from their hidings only to be massacred and buried in open graves.

A Court of Conscience

"Kalashnikov in the Sun" by Tatafway Tumoe is the first poem to attract the attention of the instrument of war in the anthology, for the simple reason that it speaks to the theme and to the instruments of a dirty war:

> It is a Kalashnikov
> a rusty piece of imported death
> lying in the sand…

At once the tone of the poem is abrupt and direct. Kalashnikov also known as AK47 is the most used weapon in African wars (imported from Russia) because it's cheap to acquire particularly in the international dirty black or white market. Considering the millions of AK47s used in African conflicts and wars, they must have fetched trillions of dollars for the Russian economy (never mind the African economy or Africa's chronic persistent food hunger!) The government did not even bother to procure modern, workable arms, but did supply the military rusty instruments to use.

What if the rust cut into the flesh of the soldiers? And in many instances they did. Did not that oversight suggest that the leaders wished for all fighters die of tetanus? What a dirty intention. To think that the imported death of instrument suggest that there were rogue international businesspeople who transacted for the purpose of killing unsuspecting citizens.

Musu Sandy captures that concept in a poem called "Hypocrisy."

> This underground denial
> Our tubers entangle in the roots
> They pour tears for brothers in distant lands
> As they replay the times of their oppressors:
> Revolution.

Musu Sandy was one of two female poets who joined our group of interwar writers, the other being Sydnella Shooter—both were founding members. Sandy was a teacher and during the war, she feared to leave her daughter at home; she carried her to school every day. She had for long sensed a murky environment, even in a benign state, when the war was only just a rumor.

The opening of the poem shows how painful the experience

is that "underground denial" of service of free talk. Perez-Pena (2005) refers to that condition as "Grumpiness." Complete ignorance that there might be a problem? Whatever it was, the lack of credible information of how the war was became a concern. Information was certainly the tubers, wires of communication, and the roots, the government "are together entangled. What a hopeless situation for citizens locked in war."

Kosonike Koso-Thomas calls his poem "Conspiracy." At that time, the human rights/wrongs situation were being flouted at will, a condition described rhetorically regarding the victims of the dirty war:

> I heard him shout
> Human sounding refrains in pain
> forced from constricted throats
> Can they hear?
> Do they know its conspiracy?

The power of his expression, "from constricted throats," conspires to uphold the human condition in torturous end. The poem goes on to describe what vulnerable citizens suffered when indiscriminately their places of worship and abodes were set on fire for withholding information from the rogue and dirty authorities of war.

What was more painful was the poem "Scars of War" in which Jonathan Kpakiwa manifested his disturbance and his visible state and traumatized being. He asks,

> They say the war is over
> The guns are silent
> What about mine in me?
> Aint my mind a chamber of war?

The war had been so dirty that even the victim feels the warfare inside, and the tendency was that it was making perpetrated citizens a clone of war. The effectiveness of the diction, chamber, demonstrates the longevity of pain, torture, and calculated attempt at bringing down the integrity of an entire personality to a beast of unreasoning.

In "My Roots in Flames" by Sydnella Shooter, Kpakiwa completes that stoicism when Shooter writes,

> Blood can't quench the fire
> weeping through my blood
> There is no fame in these flames
> But ash that brings pain
> Ash with a stain
> The ash of the slain."

Shooter has an extraordinary power of imagination that allows her to multiply and to solidify ash as a technic of double entendre. Moses Kainwo's political cum war poem "The Rare Rulers" captures the stench in a dirty war. Without a consideration of the dignity of human beings, the rulers bring into the lives of people, a rotten governance and stench of war in which:

> As if the people are paper
> They rule with a ruler
> The gun as red-ink pen
> Thunders decrees from dawn on dusk
> And the people become paper.

It's intriguing how Kainwo pictures a toddler on a school desk sketching with a red pen, guided by a ruler, a foot rule, a picture of an ink cup dripping ink or splattered:

> On the bodies of rulers
> Will instantly change their address.

We can imagine the usual end of private residencies, places of worships, or even schools on fire.

The unique reference to Oumar Farouk Sesay's poem "At

Tellu Bongor" tells of the experience of the death of sixty three civilians massacred by the rebels of the Revolutionary United Front. By this time, during the war, the rebellion of the RUF was not only unpopular, but also was not advancing any acceptable reason as to why the rebellion was bent on seizing political position other than greed. In penning the poem, Sesay has a number of questions that speak to the state of his mind and the mind of his country. He engages on a tirade of linguistic concerns as he tries to understand:

> WHAT batters, bruises, burns, blister like an
> intifada in the Gaza strips of my mind is potent hate
> battering bruising, burning, blistering to blister you
> to hell for dismembering limbs at Tellu Bongor."

The tongue twisting rapidity of the questioning in metrical succession suggests the desperation to seek for answers for what happened to deserve sixty three people to die at Tellu Bangor. The poet compares with the massacre of innocent soul to daily lives into which people in the Gaza strips are subjected.

Since the publication of *Songs That Pour the Heart*, many more individual collections of poems have gone on to spring up, specifically with the fire of the theme of war and its consequences. With the emergence of a symbolic "national" publishing company called Sierra Leone Writers Series (SLWS), there is no stopping of newer voices from emerging, a condition the president of FPS had hoped for and dreamed about in his forward of the above named anthology.

Blood on the Splattered Face of Conflict Diamonds

"The diamond trade is secretive; perhaps more secretive than any other," warned Smillie, in his compelling account, *Blood on the Stone*, aforementioned and quoted from. Is it appropriate to make an analogy that equates the greed for blood diamonds to the greed for fur from animal hair? I might have liked to ask the author if he were more than a book man or a paper man.

I couldn't help seeing the front blurb that read referring to the worth of the book, describing it as "A devastating, important work. Read this before you buy another diamond," wrote Greg Campbell. There is always a way with writers playing on meta-messages. Prince Dowu Palmer, a Sierra Leonean wrote a novel, *The Mocking Stones* about diamonds. In one scary thought, I visualize to myself that we have decided that the diamond trade is secretive, that the diamond is a devil you don't want to buy and now the diamond is a mocking stone.

By the time Naomi Campbell came on the scene, too much water had passed under the bridge with regards to conflict, blood diamonds, and the Sierra Leonean war. Internationally speaking, the scandal only added to the woes of the country. Once again, thanks to Charles Taylor, the notorious warlord, the end was only beginning. The question was then, how deep was the involvement of the country of Sierra Leone in blood diamond? Wasn't blood smeared over our country's diamonds since 1930s? The confusion regularly came when the news reportage failed to distinguish between the war fueling war and the conflict emanating from the war fueling mining diamonds.

Diamonds were discovered in Sierra Leone in the 1930s, and it only seemed that the industry was controlled selfishly under the colonial British Government, but very soon, illicit mining became quite rampant. After independence, the British Government left Sierra Leone, and the diamond trade became a free for all enterprise, thriving under the noses of corrupt politicians and local authorities. Thus, the ground becoming porous, making it possible for illicit networks disgruntled with the political establishment, a source of funding, rallied young people, gave them guns, and, changing over the power dynamics. Research showed "we first find that, beyond riots and protests, mining-induced violence is also composed of battles perpetrated by fighting groups, a form of organized violence that can lead to a change of territory (Berman et al, 2010).

Because of the deteriorating economic condition of Sierra Leone, it was not known how nobody could expect a large scale war over one fueled by conflict. One researcher, Bujra (2002) found, "Most of these rural conflicts over land and cattle have been going on over a long period, with very little attention given to them. Even today most such conflicts go unnoticed and unreported—unless large-scale killing and injuries takes place and the state intervenes militarily."

Tatafway Tumoe's poem, "Diamond Rhapsody" captures the theme of blood diamonds. If people are familiar with the area of birth of the poet, Kono, the diamondiferous place, they would not be surprised why. Strikingly, the opening verse foreshadows the events concerning Naomi Campbell or her kind. Currently, a diamondiferous lady is being addressed:

> Lady
> That quivering
> Ruby
> Dancing
> Shaking
> Glittering
> Around your graceful neck
> Was toiled
> From my tattered land.

How dare the poet accuse the lady and the diamond? The rest of the poem goes on to narrate that diamond is indeed a cursed ornament that is from the poet's land and that whenever the lady puts on the diamond he hopes that she remembers:

> the people
> The land
> The desolate hopes
> And the broken hearts
> Even though this stone
> May make you a Queen."
> Poetry of Clean War and Peace Diamond

Salute to the Remains of a Peasant (2007) is a collection of poems written by Umar Farouk Sesay, a founding member of Falui Poetry Society. His poems echo the dawn of ten years of hostilities and his collection's attempts to account the cost. Sesay sent me his work when it was only a manuscript, and he wanted me to provide the blurb. I had written for it:

> Among the poets of my generation, Umar Farouk Sesay stands out as the most lyrical—reaching us more in sounds than in words. In this collection, Sesay redefines the devices of onomatopoeia and assonance, poem after poem, with new semantic flavor. The ten-year-old war of the Sierra Leone war and that country's overall disastrous past serves as an accompanying instrument, helping him to dig deeper in the remnant of the life of the wretched, and indeed into our collective and often abused humanity wherever. Reading Sesay's poetry is like witnessing the ebb and tide of human struggle in a past and present that will never again be a foreign country.

President and founder member, Moses Kainwo who everyone agreed provided an exceptional interwar leadership both literary and managerial in terms of encouraging the membership to be creative and to keep hope alive, published his *Ayo Ayo Ayo and other Love Songs* in 2015. In his comment to the collection, the Sierra Leonean scholar, Ernest Cole, noted that the collection is:

> …personal authentic, and incisive. Written with poetic fervor and sophistication, it highlights the thematic and stylistic preoccupations of the writer in the context of pain, violence, and recovery. The poems reflected a degree of conviction and sense of commitment that suggest new directions and possibilities in Sierra Leonean literature."

It is fascinating to note that Kainwo's publication continues with the metaphor of songs, the spirit of the anthology of 2004, and the founding resolve that solidified the society. How exhilarating and reassuring to find out even after the ten-year wanton destruction that shook the fabric of the country's value system, Kainwo could write courageously in the poem, "The New Salone Leone" that:

> Sure enough
> The Salone Leone will grow taller
> Than the tallest coconut tree
> On your heart.

How creative to address the country by its alias, Salone before the name of its currency of value, "Leone" specifically addressing part of its official last name. Such a literary mechanical device emphasizes the reconciliatory tone and the willingness of all citizens to fudge ahead in the great mundane movement.

Mohamed Gibril Sesay, another founding member of the society, published a collection of poems, *At the Gathering of Roads* that has a strong metaphor of bewilderment of a people who suddenly came to the realization, leading to the significance of gathering in the village square where roads meet. At once, by that action, the people are migrating toward the centerpiece of the gathering of roads. In the poem of the title of the collection, the community resolve is well on its way to understanding that

> The strings of memories
> That bind us
> Grow so thin
> They become invisible
> Even to ourselves.

How dramatic to discover unexpectedly at the gatherings of roads that whatever strings had been visible in all its sociological limitations were broken off from their restrictions.

Along the Peal of Drums is the first collection of Ambrose

Massaquoi, another founder member of the society. The back cover of his collection reads:

> Along the Peal of Drums Ambrose Massaquoi demonstrates why he's been a dominant voice across the landscape of Sierra Leonean poetry since the early 1990s this is the oeuvre—an inventively crafted repertoire of poems evocative of the lived days and nights within the kaleidoscope of his country's story. Throughout these diverse ranges of poems, Massaquoi originates images and rhythms in ways that will drive his readers everywhere to wander and dance.

Certainly, Massaquoi has distinguished himself as a deeply moral poet whose lines seek to address the ethical being of man and society.

Founding member, Gbanabom Hallowell's *Drumbeats of War* was his first collection of poems. World renowned retired scholar, Eldred Durosimi Jones wrote about the collection:

> The spirit of search pervades the whole collection with recurring images of the poet looking through windows into vast expanses of landscape and seascape, into the Lion Mountains of his country, into its trees, listening to the sound of its rivers, its birds and its people. [Gbanabom Hallowell] peers into the dark liquid of the calabash to discover clues to the way forward, but the calabash often gets broken and like the other recurring images of the mirror which looks into the poet and outwards into the world its broken fragments have to be painfully pieced together in an effort to present the whole picture of his vision.

Conclusion

Day in day out, I regret to be reminded by the loss of Tatafway Tumoe, a founding member of the society and a literary enthusiast. His friends who knew him well called him Fway in short. Headstrong and quick to act, Tumoe was a literary genius who was not able to realize the full extent of his literary dexterity. The demands of journalism took much of his time, although he detested the political establishment which he felt did nothing to stave off the growing trade in blood diamonds in his Kono hometown.

Shortly after he passed, Mohamed Gibrl Sesay invited me one day to go with him to pay respect at the home of the recently deceased poet cum journalist. While eulogizing him, we decided to find out whether any of the relatives kept manuscripts of his writings. They promised to look, but no word has reached of the finding of any stack of manuscripts. I know that especially in the war era, Tatafway always turned in scraps of papers with poems to read. He has enough poems, at least for a collection. But we promise we would dig deep to unearth the beauty of his voice?

Several years after the end of the war, an American, Kirsten Rian, announced to the literary community that she was in Sierra Leone to work on an anthology of Sierra Leonean poets based on the experiences of the war. After much effort, she was able to publish the book. The titled of the anthology was drawn from a poem by Tatafwy Tumoe, *Kalashnokov in the Sun* (2009). Here I print the complete poem:

Kalashnikov in the Sun
by Tatafway Tumoe

It is a kalashnikov,
A rusty piece of imported
                      Death
lying in the sand.
A creeper advances

        slowly
    slowly
in the black tunnel of its barrel;
an ant walks on the trigger
a lizard suns itself on the butt.

Think with
Me;

Tangled
we move in
    barbed thoughts
endless labyrinths
    of sorrowful slogans
we die in the abstract
couched in statistics…
and yet we tighten our belts.

Think with
Me;
The crack of Kalashnikov,
lays another soldier
        down,
General eat words
from coffers of aid
        to save whom
        some ask
and pay for asking.

Where is joy,
clean clear joy
in the this land of my dreams?

In this land
where death is imported
to feed the hungry.

If guns could make us grow
we would be strutting giants
But
inflation sticks like fish-bones
in our throat
and the land still sprouts hunger.

We still need doses of aid
we tighten
our hungry stomachs
to satisfy the prophets
of inflation.

Let us make the belly-full
of kola nuts
and then beat the kalashnokov
impotent as weapons,
turn them into hoes
machetes and pick-axes
and go turning and tilling
the soil anew.

Tatafway Tumoe was not a political statesman. He lived his life simply and died unknown, save for the lines he wrote here and there; lines we hope someday someone will say that there they are, *The Manuscripts of Tatafway Mani Tumoe*. Until then, Oumar Farouk has chosen to remember his poet friend, Fway with the following lines:

Tumoe

Tatafway Mani Tumoe wrote the final line
of a life lacerated by many lies
like rash strokes on canvas.
Now he had crossed the ultimate line

> to stand in line in the eternal line.
> For him all lines have fused to a single line;
> Timelelines and deadlines are dead like death.
> We mourn him as we wait in line tied to timeliness
> to cross the ultimate line to be in line
> with Tatafway Mani Tumoe.

Other founding members, Musu Sandy, Sydnella Shooter, and Ousman Barrie in the local or international community remain in view, but they have either veered here and there into other interests while keeping creative writing on the side. Keeping in mind that while life would need to be diversified, there are members who write poetry occasionally, and when they find the time to write, they are excited. They know where to find the society to have their work included in any anthology.

For a country where there is no functional national bookshop anywhere, where the national libraries are grossly underfunded, where the school authorities primary, secondary, or tertiary do not encourage literary creativity, where the national creative process is neither funded nor granted publication subsidies to stimulate the welfare of creativity in the way of growth, it is important that I keep my testament of an interwar poetry group that made me an apprentice of writing

References

Berman et al (2010). "This mine is mine! How minerals fuel conflicts in Africa" Retrieved Friday June 14, 2019.

Bujra, Abdallah. (2002). "African Conflicts: Their Causes and Their Political and Social Environment,"

Campbell, G. (2010) blurb from front cover of Blood on the Stone by Ian Smillie (2010) *Blood on the stone: Greed, corruption and war in the global diamond trade*. Anthem Press.

Dictionary.com https://www.dictionary.com/ (Tuesday August 06, 2019)

Giusti, Franchesca (2019). "Resitation" https://www.ici- berlin.org/oa/ci-15/giusti_recitation.pdf
Retrieved June 14, 2019

Perez-Pena, Richard. (2005). "Confidence underground. Or Was that Denial?" New York Times
nytimes.com/2005/12/15/nyregion/nyregionspecial3/confidence-underground-or-was-that-denial.html

Retrieved August 8, 2019
Smillie, Ian. (2010). *Blood on the stone: Greed, corruption and war in the global diamond trade:* Anthem Press.
Sesay, Mohamed G. & Kainwo, Moses (2004). Songs That Pour the Heart New Initiatives Publishing.
Sesay, Oumar F. (2004). "THE Poetics of resilience" An account of the opening of the Special Court of Sierra Leone.

CHAPTER 2

Manufacturing Mocking Stones: A Philosophical Review of De Caprio's *Blood Diamond*

"Sometimes I wonder whether God will forgive us for what we have done to each other. God left this place a long time ago."

> Danny Archer as portrayed by Leonardo de Caprio

Finda was born in Kono, Sierra Leone's famous diamond town. She is 18 years old and has never set eyes on a diamond. Although most of her relatives live, breathe, and thirst for diamonds and fantasize all the time to her about how the family would shake the pillars of the earth with wealth the day they happen upon a giant stone. Today, Finda is seeing a diamond for the first time. Her unassuming *Poomweh*, American lover, whose mission to Sierra Leone she never cares to find out, places a sand-like object in her palm.

Meanwhile, her relatives continue to bask in chronic, persistent poverty. Poomweh places the stone in Finda's palm and says to her, "What you are holding is a diamond."

Not knowing what to believe, she considers the stone for a while and emotionlessly replies, "Is it the object that has all the force to it?"

In the night while excitedly having sex, Finda allows her body and soul to concentrate on the affair, making it possible to carve a charm in in the heart of the American that would send Poomweh hurriedly the next morning, to file the papers that would allow her to travel to the United States, the country in her dream that, could be the only place where "diamonds" really grow into trees.

When he had had the chance, Poomweh had gone for the ultimate erotica associated with the pleasures of finality, wealth, and accomplishment. And when the two had separated from the affair, Poomweh realized that the possibility of their paths crossing again would be one in a million chances.

There are a million unassuming Westerners roving through the streets of Africa in time of war or peace, all looking deeply into the bottom of vulnerable countries and waiting to find diamonds and other precious stones. A million more Middle Easterners, mostly Syrians and Lebanese, are sitting in front of shops and coordinating the dirty affair of illicit mining under the noses of African leaders, who sign papers of legitimacy for these Martians of predators. By the same mathematical token, thousands of unschooled, unfed, uncared-for underage boys are shaking the wash-pans in large awkward pits by day and by night to search out diamonds for their impatient abusers.

Whatever the reason for making the movie, *Blood Diamond*, an ambitious, atomizing creation, the producers (more in purpose) failed to delay the cameras to capture the first port of human rights abuse, only glossing over the wash-pan shaking boys and instead dwelled on war captive and diamond slave, Solomon Vandi and his discovery of a large diamond he skillfully hid between his toes and later buried in a place only he knew. In search of this treasure, the picture zoomed to the white foreign merchant, Danny Archer (Leonardo de Caprio) visiting war torn Sierra Leone and who had gotten wind of Solomon's diamond and would dare in every bloody scene to reach the stone.

The trouble with *Blood Diamond* is that its metaphorical substance as promised in its title sags under a mundane storyline. A movie carrying such a metaphorical and pregnant title should have several anecdotes of antithetical episodes added to its storyline because real conflicts are results of human paradoxes. Instead, what we see are two storylines: one of civil conflict not properly developed and another of dirty business deals, and both stories fail to intertwine. This situation calls into question as to whether Hollywood is insinuating that the Sierra Leone civil conflict was fought over diamonds, or was fueled by diamonds. But of course the movie did not provide an answer.

Meanwhile, in the daily wait for diamonds, merchants and warlords, to kill the time and coax their impatience, continue to pull the virgin skirts of the many unsuspecting Findas, pouring into their flesh only to draw out the first blood of defilement. Every so often, cases of this nature occur in the heartland of Angola, Sierra Leone, and the DRC. While the diamondiferous relationships that forge between the white foreign merchants and the indigenes glitter with radiance—but lack goodwill.

Let us immediately bring in the circumstances of the ethic of justice to our narration. All the while, we have in mind the metaphor of blood as we follow Danny Archer, the white merchant, and Solomon Vandi, the local farmer turned digger of diamonds, into the pit where the dialogue of exploitation has made bedfellows of people with nothing in common, only that one of the two, Archer (the Westerner) is reaching to exploit in the name of goodwill, while Vandi, the other, as a dog in a manger (the Southerner) knowing not how to lie in.

John Rawls, the philosopher, refers to the relationship I have described above as "the subjective circumstance," and, in this case, the diamonds in the south, a possession of the Africans, and an envy of the Westerners, have humbled the two to associate, albeit in a strange bedfellow manner. What metaphor of blood can we discern in relationships of subjective circumstances? The connotation to blood here is similar to the one I made above about merchants and innocent Findas. In discussing subjective circumstance further, Rawls wrote, "The plans and conceptions of good, lead them (parties) to have different ends and purposes," and to make conflicting claims to the natural and social resources available.

In this regard, the good *Samaritanism* of Archer is at once problematic. He presents himself as a man concerned about helping Vandi trace back and reunite with his family, but his real intention is to locate Vandi's diamond buried somewhere that only Vandi knows the location. At once, it is clear that an absence of conceptions of good is itself a recipe for disaster. Thus, in this case, we can push Rawls' quotation further to talk about bad blood and good blood.

Further down the page, Mill made a point that undermines the goodwill effort of Archer and the moralizing of (Hollywood) West, appropriate to the international circumstances surrounding African conflict diamonds. Mill wrote that the utilitarian morality does recognize in human beings the power of sacrificing their own greatest good for the good of others. It only refuses to admit that the sacrifice is itself good. A sacrifice which does not increase or tend to increase the sum total of happiness is considered as wasted.

A number of false paradigms run through the movie that collectively negate the first half of Mill's statement. Archer opting to help Vandi reunite with his family cannot be reasoned as a man given to utilitarian morality. It is ironical that, Archer who has by now become the quintessential American, gun slinging hero could kill other Africans at will and without the slightest camera-image of remorse. But also and perhaps more importantly, is that while the metaphor of blood is glaring in the African fields, in (Hollywood) West, the movie downplays reality. It instead "manufactures," and creates a haven of sane men (only capable of existing outside Africa so to speak) of sound judgment away from the troubled continent, who care about the atrocities related to diamonds on the African continent. There are greedy faces in the West, of conglomerate interest on whom the camera should have turned, to capture their miserly relationships to African diamonds if the metaphor of blood and the genesis of the conflict were really intended to be exposed. Therefore, in utilitarian terms, the sacrifice is problematic, being that it is both not good and also wasted.

When the ultimate result of morality becomes only of deontological concern, then the goodness in the will Kant is concerned about, can only be enjoyed, and even then, not in any utilitarian manner, by the inanimate concepts of duty and the laws; Of what good is it then thus conflicting with the theory that the laws are made for men and not men for the laws. If nations and institutions are going to be adamantly deontological, if their laws are not made dynamic on behalf of the utilitarian needs of humanity what then is the future of ethical morality? So that, as Kant argued, even where good will meets with a stormy threat and the fatal process of destruction, humanity must rejoice because good will, characteristic of its fullness of virtue "would spark like a jewel all by itself, as something that had its full worth in itself."

Kant reminds us of the biblical story of the Christ, who performed acts of miracles on the Sabbath, purely out of a Kantian good will, but would still be condemned by Kantian Pharisees. Indeed, deontological ethics in its strictest sense can be an enemy of utilitarianism, the only ethic that is a virtue in itself.

In talking about utilitarianism as a superior virtue to other human values, a consideration regarding its misuse can be a counter-argument. Kant argued, "The more a cultivated reason deliberately devotes itself to the enjoyment of life and happiness, the more the man falls short of true contentment." The problem with this assumption can be understood from a couple of angles. First, Kant in using "cultivated reason" and "deliberately devotes" to mean to deconstruct every element of sanity attached to utilitarianism and, in its stead, reconstruct a concept of drunkenness and lust. To my mind, Kant is confusing uncontrolled desire with happiness; but even if it is rational to imagine that pleasure/happiness can be abused, it is equally imaginable that goodwill can be falsified.

In *Blood Diamond* several acts of goodwill are falsified. Of paramount example is the ulterior motive of reaching a hidden diamond that is attached in Archer's conditionality to help Vandi locate his family. After all, Vandi was only one of many farmers who had lost his family in the usual rebel raid in the Sierra Leone civil conflict. In that case, goodwill, as Kant believes, it cannot be said to be *perfectly* good in itself. And as Mill rightly stated, "The creed which accepts as the foundation of morals Utility or the Greatest Happiness Principle holds that actions are right in proportion as they tend to promote happiness, but wrong as they tend to produce the reverse of happiness."

In the case of *Blood Diamond*, these acts of "goodwill" motivated by greed can only create and deepen the curse of conflict that the movie purports to correct. Mill is accepting the usually productive and counter-productive theory of the philosopher's circle that sees a progression of an act of sanity, often gravitating from its earliest form and moving toward an improved and complex situation. However, when such progression continues until it reaches its original point, where the matter is already problematic, it is usually as a result of a counter-productive development. This situation is what Mill refers to as a tendency to "produce the reverse of happiness," something long observed by Bentham, thereby leading him to re-evaluate the earliest concept of utilitarianism and, thus considering any abuse of happiness, a pain to be avoided.

The following advice by Rawls cannot be more appropriate for anyone than the Hollywood filmmakers of *Blood Diamond*. We want to define the original position so that we get the desired solution. If knowledge of particulars is allowed, then the outcome is biased by arbitrary contingencies. As already observed, to each according to his threat advantage is not a principle of justice. If the original position is to yield agreements that are just, then the parties must be fairly situated and treated equally as moral persons. The arbitrariness of the world must be corrected by adjusting the circumstances of the initial contractual situation.

Blood Diamond, as I have mentioned above, is problematic in the respect Rawls is quoted. A movie project undertaken to examine the conflict over diamonds ought to be as universal as the problem itself. Where, for instance, is the picture of the scheming carried out by the buyers of diamonds in the West, a situation itself that, in reality has exacerbated the conflict over diamonds? Are rogue diamond businesses not in reality part of the diamond conflict? Is the blood on the African field not being spilled as a result of the big dollars of the West ready to negotiate on illicit terms? A naïve but simple truth is that the Africans butchering each other on the diamond fields have not exhibited any willingness or readiness and the technology to transform a raw diamond into anything beyond its crude form in the way that western technology can.

Aristotle seeks to examine justice in light of human interpersonal relationships. Like he does with all other human values, Aristotle speaks of the equitable nature of justice. He shifts the argument to a global viewpoint; he is interested in atomizing justice on a global platform. He wrote, "Now the laws in their enactments on all subjects aim at the common advantage either of all or the best of those who hold power, or something of the sort; so that in one sense we call those acts just that tend to produce and preserve happiness and its components for the political good."

Kant reminds us that "morals themselves remain subject to all kinds of corruption so long as the guide and supreme norm for their correct estimation is lacking." The closure of *Blood Diamond* is problematic in the Kantian sense of the word. In the movie, people of the philanthropic West are in a conference to decide on the moral problems related to the conflict over diamonds. It is the conviction of the men who meet in the round table that regulating the sale of diamonds in the West will minimize the conflict in Africa; again, the moral problems show because the international (or cross boundary) fault lines are not all identified.

It does not occur to the round table men, or they do not acknowledge that, while the western diamondiferous jewelry buyer could be a passive party to the conflict, (even that assumption is faulty because the buyer by law could be criminalized), the Western diamond companies are themselves active participants to it. As an addendum, on the wake of the movie, there was the urgent move by Western diamond companies, taking large and expensive advertising spaces in print and electronic media to disassociate themselves from conflict diamonds. Such adverting comes about on two fraudulent platforms: first, the adverts are not intended for an African audience or are made to sympathize with African victims, but to appease the Western buyers of diamondiferous jewelries. Second, the campaign advertizing adds to the Hollywood capitalistic ploy of falsifying the fact that the blood attached to diamonds is a universal pandemic perpetrated by peoples of all continent, particularly so the imperialist market economy of the west.

In the movie, no African value is sought in identifying and resolving the conflict over diamonds. Perhaps an inclusion of African diplomats in the West in the round table toward the end, might have posed the true challenge to matters of universal ethics regarding conflict diamonds.

Toward the end of the movie, the *pedestrialization* of Vandi in the West is meant to compliment the moral ideology of the West and not to consult with its African counterpart, or any southern ideology of morality for that matter, as to how to combat the global conflict over diamonds.

As mankind goes into the 21st century, cross cultural exchanges occupy center stage in the international arena. The global village with its imperialist elements depends on the good conduct of human communication to succeed. But every so often, the communication tools meet with disconnects, thus making us mankind go crazy with each other for reading "our" symbols wrong. We are quick to forget that we come to the table with our individual national, local, and personal symbols and, no, we had not completely merged them to those of a universal culture. Now, time we are in conflictual situations, we go back to our reservoir of personal and national cultures to help us find responses. *Blood Diamond* could have been a better movie had Hollywood taken multi-cultural issues into consideration. For the most part, the conflicts we have with others coming from different orientations submerge, leaving us disputants with different (mis)perceptions in the relationships.

Today, societies all over the world are haunted by acts of sadism, an element itself undercutting world peace. The profit motif enriches Hollywood, among giant movie industries, and at the same time, draining the mental and material capacities of governments and societies. Utilitarianism is gradually becoming an exit option if the world must be stopped from collapsing into the proverbial black hole. I posit that all human values, be they goodwill or justice, are not only secondary in importance and a means to utilitarianism, but they are conceptually limited in time and place. For instance an American goodwill in Iraq is not necessarily shared by the Iraqi resistant movement; and the moral/ethical justification for a suicidal bomber in Iraq may not culturally and otherwise be appreciated in the West). Utilitarianism can be a means to itself and an end in itself, that is, in addition to being a universal value.

In conclusion, it is important to comment on the surprising twist and closure of the movie. *Blood Diamond* is hardly about the curse of diamonds in Sierra Leone, for events in the movie only comfortably pave a path for the West to seek self-gratification in its policing of world matters. Nel Noddings argued that "…an ethic of caring locates morality primarily in the pre-act consciousness of the one caring." For it is shocking to see that Archer, who from the beginning of the movie has exhibited every scheming ploy he can, such as impersonating journalists and relief workers, with the sole aim of reaching the hidden diamond of Vandi, could all at once emerge as a human rights crusader and articulate the cause of a country and people, whose vulnerability he is shown to deeply understand and has plundered over and over. This literary quick-fix of falsity speaks volumes about the moral integrity of the storyline and the "original intention" Rawls talked about.

Blood Diamond would have succeeded had it not attempted such a trite and mono-focal solution to the complex problems associated with the trafficking of diamonds and other precious stones. For instance, what are the Sierra Leone government policies regarding the international sale of diamonds to international buyers? Did anybody care to include them in the movie? How well did Hollywood care to research issues of legitimacy as per Sierra Leone's legal system on the ownership of diamonds the size Vandi discovered? Is it reality when Vandi trotted the streets of London negotiating for his diamond? Why did Hollywood abandon the above concerns? The answer is clear in the estimation of Hollywood ethics can only be universal when its values are western. But of course that's not true.

Perhaps the turning point in the movie comes about after Archer handed over the rediscovered diamond to Vandi, knowing that his own life was threatened by a deepening gunshot wound from a skirmish with a corrupt UN backed foreign military team operating in Sierra Leone. The short conversation that ensued between Solomon and Archer after Archer had handed over the diamond draws attention to the global presence in the Sierra Leone conflict over diamonds:

> Solomon Vandi: (on receiving the diamond) I thought you would steal it from me.
> Danny Archer: (with paining laughter). It occurred to me…eh!"

It is my opinion, that while the demise of Archer attracts sympathy and for the first time in the movie gives voice to the Sierra Leonean side, it complicates the storyline, leaving the conflict only on a pseudo-solution axis. In London, a now wealthy and secured Vandi is called upon by the high table philanthropists to articulate on conflict diamonds, and it becomes clear that the movie, rather than ending, only then attempts to confront the reality of the universal problems posed by conflict diamonds. As the camera zooms on Vandi, dressed in European suits (I wish he had worn Sierra Leonean national attire. But is not Hollywood wishing to make a point about how the West can refine an African personality as perfectly as a crystal peace diamond ring?). Walking to the podium, I re-echo with satisfaction the last words of caution given by a philanthropist in the movie: "Let us learn from that (Vandi's voice) and let us ignore it no more!" Is the world listening? Is there anything of value for and from Sierra Leone? Yes, the note of irony and the mischaracterization in the movie. Never mind.

References

Archer & Vandi. (2006). *Blood Diamond*, Hollywood Movie.

Aristotle. (1861). "Utilitarianism" in Philosophical Classics; From Plato to Nietzsche. (ed) Forrest Baird and Walter Kaufmann. (1997). Prentice Hall: New Jersey. P.992.

Kant, I. (1785). "Foundation for the Metaphysics of Morals" in Philosophical Classics; From Plato to Nietzsche. (ed) Forrest Baird and Walter Kaufmann. (1997). Prentice Hall: New Jersey. P.900.

Mill, J.S. (1861). "Utilitarianism" in Philosophical Classics; From Plato to Nietzsche. (ed) Forrest Baird and Walter Kaufmann. (1997). Prentice Hall: New Jersey. P.992.

Noddings, N. (1995). "Ethics and Caring" in Justice and Care: Essential Readings in feminist Ethics. Westview Press: Colorado. P.9.

Rawls, John. (1971). A Theory of Justice. Harvard University Press: Cambridge

Chapter 3

African Verse and the Cultural Forces of World Poetry

I do not write about the culture of versification in poetry in the rhythmical sense, but rather with a geographical, linguistic, and emotional interpretive analysis. I want to associate versification with the accents of oral speech. Versification in poetry makes for a poem's exclusive "non-otherness" when compared to other kinds of poetry. Anthropologists, for instance, tend to think of culture as divided into high and low contexts, meaning collectivists and individualists respectively. Western and African poetry have developed their accents of versification accordingly. A simple formula for the distinction is conceptualized in how Western poetry is "I & me" oriented, while African poetry is "we & us" oriented. I shall return to this issue later.

At times, Western poetry, particularly American poetry, tends to accompany Western politics abroad by way of policing world literature. The British had that role (proselytizing, but not policing) long ago until the Americans rose to the center of world order and changed the face of politics from an empirical outlook to capitalistic framing. In modern times, during the reign of Shakespeare's much younger cousins, Yeats and others, America sent a batch of missionary poets abroad. Those who made inroads into Africa included Walt Whitman, Robert Frost, and others. While these poets didn't sound much different from their British counterparts, they, nevertheless, occupied the African literary scene with a forceful political nature. I have heard it said in many quarters, literary and otherwise, that African poetry did not develop an accent of its own until the complete enslavement, colonization, and neo-colonization of African poetics by Western poetry—(the Western poets themselves have nothing to do with this political conquistador arrangement). What then does it mean to say that African poetry did not develop an accent of its own? To imply, as stated above, however, is to suggest that regarding African poetics, there was originally only poetry of silence before the big bang!

At the MFA in Writing program at Vermont College, I met many fine American poets—sometimes, among them were European poets also—all of whom occasionally cut across in their poetry with beautiful lines referencing some African images. However, further discussion with these poets usually solicited only grand innocence of a continent that has breathed its unique versification into poetry since its creation. To many of these poets, Africa does not exist as a continent of soil and water, but only in their modern imagination as otherness. Being the only black student at Vermont College at the time, for that matter, being an African reading my way into American poetry, I felt poetically estranged.

I approached contemporary American poetry with the accent of contemporary African poetry. When I read David St. Joan, I echoed David Rubadiri; when I encountered Charles Bukowski, I saw Dambudzo Marechera; and when I examined Lynn Emmanuel, I visualized Patricia Jabbeh Wesley. For two years as a student poet, I found the traffic of poetry too heavy on my way. At the time, I had also discovered Cesar Vallejo and Pablo Neruda, both of whom wrote with quite other forms of versification: the Latin American forms of versification. Because exile has a way of growing a solitary tree in the heart, I found solace in the surrealism of Latin American poetry. As bad luck would have it, North America hated abstract poetry. Because I was an exile, unless I wrote via the culture of the host, my abstraction was going to remain *abstract*. Adrienne Rich, an American poet, captures one such probable clash in a similar setting:

> I had bought a dress with a too-long skirt. The shop employed a seamstress who did alterations, and she came in to pin up the skirt on me. I am sure that she was a recent immigrant, a survivor. I remember a short, dark woman wearing heavy glasses, with an accent so foreign I could not understand her words. Something about her presence was very powerful and disturbing to me.

What was it about this immigrant woman's presence that was "very powerful and disturbing" to Rich? Sometimes, when we cannot easily permeate a cultural divide, we see everything about it as making no sense, yet the silent wall holds a sacred stillness that transmits a powerful newness even of the unknown and the undiscovered. The poetic experience makes for an even more disturbing case: readers of a "foreign" work of poetry first have to accede to certain internal alterations before they can pass through the abstraction. Reading a work that is culturally challenging requires a deeply interactive process. Perhaps the first step requires the poet and the reader to *demystify* the meeting. The next step calls for honesty. An open door policy is the guiding principle for a truly universal relationship.

I considered American poetics in a similar fashion. I came into American poetry as a survivor. I left Africa with only one dream: to be a poet in America. I have since encountered one big problem in my dreaming, and that is to be a poet in America! Part of the problem results from Americans not suspecting that, having arrived in exile in my mid-30s, I could only be an African poet in America and not an American poet. Like Rich's recent immigrant, I stood out in Vermont "with an accent so foreign" that hardly anyone understood my poetry. Perhaps it was the manner I had reached to pin up my poetry on the Americans, for I met with many who wanted to, but could not find me palatable. Poetry requires the patience of the reader, especially poetry with a foreign accent. In such poetry, a reader has to tread cautiously; otherwise, an unfamiliar accent can make the reading experience catastrophic!

It is important that we ask ourselves some pertinent political questions regarding the poetry we write and the poetry we read, as Louis Simpson has posed: "… does poetry have no power in itself? No reality? What would happen if instead of trying to write poetry one allowed silence to speak?" On the human survival pyramid, poetry maintains a significant place. I posit that any nation that has not produced a great tradition of poetry will certainly not boast of a healthy tradition of great novelists, dramatists, and leaders—again, this reality ought to be given political consideration. The novelist, dramatist, and leader feed on the political poesy of the poet, who enjoys the power of the trinity of god the word, god the image, and god the metaphor. Being the spiritual form of all human art, poetry establishes a people's accent upon which every other agency builds an aesthetic. Poetry could be a benevolent spirit. Although I doubt its benevolent temperament, it is indeed a spirit. However, poets who migrate beyond their cultural domain usually encounter other accents of versification that infiltrate their art. Nevertheless, they do not compromise their nurtured accents. After all, any poem that misappropriates its value system becomes "impure." The reader should be able to discover the genetic uniqueness of any one poem when a DNA-like test of it is run. Simpson succinctly summarizes this uniqueness in the following way:

> If poetry is to matter, we must put in our poems those elements that have been excluded as impure. This means breaking with the standards set by the academy, by those who have made emptiness a virtue—who have elevated Stevens above Frost, above Williams and Pound and Eliot . . .

My earliest workshop advisor at Vermont College was a seasoned poet—Jewish by orientation, American by accent of versification, and author of many exemplary poems. This poet pruned the pretentious confidence I had, with which I had walked into his Vermont College workshop, of already being a poet at ease. My advisor helped me to realize the state of my literary emergency at the time. My enjambments were a cliff I could have dropped off from; my closures, a dungeon I could have been trapped in; and my poetic license was eventually going to be revoked for ignoring the road signs on Poetry Avenue!

There are poets, and there are teacher-poets. My advisor was a teacher-poet whose technical wealth sometimes couldn't hold him back from invading other people's accents of versification. "The Dining Table" was a poem on which my advisor and I had worked back and forth for a period of two weeks. While we did not necessarily agree that the poem was finally finished, we certainly had to move on to other things in our six–month-long semester. However, just as we were about to do so, he saw one last thing! *the pepper/ strong enough to push scorpions/up our heads.* He read the line and said to me, "You know, we don't speak like that in America. We don't express it that way in the English language." This one last issue on this poem certainly placed us in the tension-filled space where colors separate. Two poets, one a teacher-poet and the other a student-poet were about to be divided by the politics of our different accents of versification. In the end I allowed the poem to appear in my first collection in my own accent of versification, the first stanza of which I have reproduced below.

> Dinner tonight comes with
> gun wounds. Our desert
> tongues lick the vegetable
> blood—the pepper
> strong enough to push scorpions
> up our heads. Guests
> look into the oceans of bowls

> as vegetables die on their tongues.

The line that separated us was, "—the pepper/strong enough to push scorpions/up our heads." My advisor, a passionate poet, grew up in a community whose culture taught him to say, "Pepper will go into your chest." I was brought up in a community whose culture taught me that "pepper goes into the head." The disagreement was not only between two words, "head" and "chest," but also between the biological, cultural, and nutritional accents of the words. Was science an argument either of us could have used in poetry to appropriate the line? Do political and scientific accuracies matter in poetry? Does falsehood in the accent of versification affect a work of poetry in world cultures? Can cultural forces undermine the universality of a poem? Can a poem *really be universal?*

Simpson talks about poets having the task of putting "into words the message that form[ed] itself out of our silence." By silence, Simpson is referring to our consciences, individuality, and biological make-up. He appropriately quotes Maria Rilke who writes, "But listen to the voice of the wind/and the ceaseless message that forms itself out of silence." A poet in exile feeds on exactly that: voice, message, and silence. Whenever poets are torn between two cultures, more like threatened by a foreign accent, a challenge is posed to them about whether they could articulate their own accents of versification for international consumption. Poets who fail to take this challenge, whether from a superior or an inferior culture too often write poems, as Joan Aleshire observes, that "are bits of filigree rather than true bridges from the poet's consciousness to the reader's, carrying essential information."

Wole Soyinka, a pioneer African poet, articulates with ease the culture into which he was born. Soyinka is a poet who, from the birth of his talent, sought a universal identity by feeding on the traditions of Western literature. At the time, literarily and culturally famished as he was, he was thoroughly bred on the Western canon in his home country of Nigeria, and in England where he studied. At the height of his education, he sought to break open his path on the backs of both his native literary oral tradition and the written tradition of the West. Soyinka, throughout his career, is not the kind of poet a critic would say developed his philosophical outlook. He rather developed his genius and instead, it could be said of him that he evolved in his cultural and philosophical outlook after he discovered his voice, so that his earlier plays and poetry, like his latter ones, have insisted only on a classification and universalization of his accent of versification. In a poem called "Dedication," he wrote:

> Shield you like the flesh of palms, skyward held
> Cuspids in thorn nesting, insealed as the heart of kernel—
> A woman's flesh is oil—child, palm oil on your tongue
> Is suppleness to life, and wine of this gourd
> From self-same timeless run of runnels as refill
> Your podlings, child, weaned from your embrace

Poets are separated one from another when the kinds of pictures they conjure help to explain a concept or a situation. How do love, hate, pressure, and anxiety run in a poet's accent of versification? What images does a poet use to heighten or reduce fear? Would a Western poet have used the expression "a flesh of palms?" What esoteric importance does "skyward held" have in Soyinka's accent of versification? Do these words transfer to a Western accent of versification? Could that expression be made a world culture? If so, does it need to carry over its esoteric meaning to be effective, or must people of other orientation only stumble upon strange accents in poems and not bother to question their esoteric presence?

Soyinka's poem is the promise of an experience, not one the persona is about to go through but one that the persona is currently going through. Discovery comes along with information. Amidst an accent of cultural images, ignorance is frightened by the face of a new dawn. Would a Westerner imagine a woman's flesh as palm oil on the tongue? Does a Westerner think about palm oil when experiencing a woman's flesh? Is a child weaned from its mother after a period of breastfeeding? Does weaning a child hold any significance in the West? In Soyinka's accent of versification, weaning a child could be cause for celebration at the family or community level. Does Soyinka want his readers to perceive any significant concepts and not just read his poem as one man would bawl a "Hi" to another on a Western, winter street? Poets, like any other professionals, have contributed to the construction of the global village; but like it is with politicians, poets rain on each other's parade. Ali Mazrui warns that "part of the price of having the world transferred into a global village is that incitement can become transterritorial."

Writers on both sides of the Atlantic reserve their opinions about poetry from the other side. Apparently, the West remains the biggest funder and promoter of all literatures. Every Asian and African writer who has won the Nobel Prize for literature probably owes the Western world a debt. The literature of the West continues to make significant in-roads into African schools and colleges. These Western books come in handy, for books written by Africans are hard to come by, even if printed in the continent. They don't circulate too well in the West either. Charles Larson captures many of the problems plaguing African writers and their writings. Among them is the following: "Books simply cost too much in Africa . . . and therefore fall within the domain of luxury items."

Abioseh Nicol, a Sierra Leonean poet, brings a deeply savannah accent of versification to African poetry. In his exilic poem, "The Meaning of Africa," Nicol discovers only the continent's "sombre green challenge" while living in the West, although he was seeking to discover the full-blooded Africa as a way of understanding the continent of his birth, which was "once just a name to me." Writing in the style of a more popular poet, David Diop, Nicol shows snippets of his Western proselytizing, which make him less knowledgeable of the Africa that he should have known all too well about. Descended from freed slaves who returned to Freetown, Sierra Leone, Nicol is familiar with only peripheral Africa. He, therefore, cautions that to discover the real Africa, his fellow Africans should

> Go up-county, so they said,
> To see the real Africa.
> For whomsoever you may be,
> That is where you come from.
> Go for bush, inside the bush,
> You will find your hidden heart,
> Your mute ancestral spirit.
> And so I went, dancing on my way.

What heightens Nicol's accent of versification in the poem is the expression, "Go for bush." Using a non-Western expression by every imagination, Nicol goes beyond the cosmetic nature of the rural African to explore Africa as an object of its forests. He describes Africa of the living as well as of the dead, Africa of ancestral essence, and Africa free of foreign values!

Richard Jackson is an exciting contemporary American poet who dares to cross the American border in order to engage foreign readers. In his poetry, Jackson circumnavigates the world, and from the recesses of ancient Europe to the natural plateaus of sub-Sahara Africa, he draws his images. His poetry asserts itself well in an African aura. Its familiar images are used in ways unfamiliar to an African. He writes in "Teiresias" that

> The sky is beautiful because it has no memory.
> The bones of the night are thinning because
> they lack sufficient calcium. There is a lot
> more I could tell you.

Certainly, the African reader who has a different perception of the sky and of the night is eager to hear more from Jackson. Africans tend to appreciate the spiritual connotation attached to the sky, that the spirit has long memory, and that the sky spews the night and swallows it also, a duty it has never failed to perform since creation. In my country for instance, people of my Themne ethnic group call the sky *kuru*, the abode of God who is called *Kru*. How can the sky therefore lack memory or the night calcium? Would Jackson have used these images in such a way if he were an African poet?

I don't need an essay this long to discuss the differences in world poetry, or to argue that African poetry did not shoot from its Western counterpart. However, the diversity in our literature is itself a literary pleasure. There is beauty in the differences between the day and the night; therefore, no matter how much we stumble in the dark, the night will scare us if it pretends to be a day. Today's poetry is different from that of yesterday's. My generation of poets, wherever they are in the world, differs from the poets of yesterday. The 21st century poets are now reaching toward writing world poetry; however, that goal doesn't detract from the various accents of versification. George Joseph wrote:

> Folklore in countries such as Italy, France, or England stands as popular literature in opposition to the written productions of an elite and indeed may be influenced by the latter. African oral literature, on the other hand, represents the aspirations of an entire people and ranges from sublime religious ideals to everyday practical advice.

Earlier in the essay, I posited that poetry is a spirit-art, and that every nation that must produce incredible novels, drama, and leaders must first produce fine poets who have built a fountain of letters. As quoted above, Joseph reminded us about the "sublime religious ideals" of indigenous African literature. African poetry can better be understood and appreciated when articulated with the help of the African drum and the African tambourine. For instance, in Senegal, the royal poet, known as the *griot*, can succeed only in articulating his poetry when his instrument agrees with him. However, if the spirit-art was not particularly given to the occasion, the audience, or the organizer, the poet, and his instrument, will not make a good duet. To say that African poetry is also African music would not be completely correct because the former does not move its audience to dance for pleasure, but causes them to chant and commune with the gods and the ancestors. It is an opportunity for the audience to spend a moment with the guardians of the community.

J.H. Nketia, a Ghanaian writer, said, "The use of drums as 'vehicles of language' is a widespread art in Africa. Drums however, are not meant to compete with human speech in ordinary everyday life, but rather to supplement in certain situations." Certainly, if the griot was not compelling in words, the drum in the hand of a "favored" player could move the gods and the ancestors. In many African communities where war and pestilence usually rob the people of their great poets for some time, the drums became the only "poets" to lead festivals and other ceremonies. It is not surprising that many poetic expressions such as "*kon kon ken ken ken*," which is interpreted as *Asamanfo, monko, monko... Akyeampon Tententen* ("spirits of the Departed"), a Ghanaian drum sound, became part of the poetic register of the land. When this development occurs, even the drummer-poet is humbled. He certainly had not achieved the moment on his own accord, for only the gods could have moved his hands to drum so well. Nketia further explains what happens:

> After that the drummer announces himself and at the close he says either "I am learning, let me succeed," or "I am addressing you, and you will understand." He then goes on to address various parts of the drum which are also "awakened" for the festival—the wood, the pegs, the skin, the string, the drum, and says to each one in turn: "I am learning, let me succeed."

He then proceeds to address the following one by one: the Earth, God, the cook, the witch, the court crier, the executioner, all past drummers, and lastly the god Tango.

In discussing the cultural forces in world poetry, I shall like to return to the issue of persons as I promised in the opening. While Western poetry is integrally personal, African poetry continues to occupy public spaces. In Africa, the poet and art are "public property," and thus remains in the service of his or her community. Whereas the African artists in other genres entertain with narration, dramatization, and graffiti, the poet appeals to the psyche. At festivals and other ceremonies, the poet and his audience are challenged to level with spirit-nature through idealistic expressions. Many American poets to whom I have spoken define poetry as a rather personal enterprise. Such is the same way their readers see the genre. A poet of homosexual orientation is almost always going to weave every experience around homosexualism; a feminist poet is always liberating a woman from the mind of a chauvinist male; and a minority poet is always going to cry foul against a bullying majority. In the West, poets are labeled, whereas in Africa only the work of poets is labeled. When an African poet writes nature poetry, it is always used as a vehicle to address a socio-political concern. Even after the numerous criticisms written on the art of African poetry, very little is known about the poets themselves. African critics have always concentrated on the works their poets produce. Leopold Sedar Senghor, Wole Soyinka, Okot p'bitek, David Diop, Tchikaya U'Tamsi, Dennis Brutus, and a host of other of Africa's finest poets have not had any significant studies done on them as a way of examining the private spaces of their lives. Haven't Frost and other nature poets been read only on a truly gardening or horticultural theme? American poets certainly conduct their enterprises as personal undertakings. Walt Whitman has the most appropriate example:

> I celebrate myself,
> And what I assume you shall assume
> For every atom belonging to me as good belongs to you

African poets are not categorically Whitmanesque in the way of American poets. In Africa, the poet celebrates the community. The poets' songs are in accordance with the pulse of their communities. Perhaps because Africa has had a history of survivalists going back to the dinosaurian struggle of repelling Arabo-European exploitation, the communal has instilled in the African the sense of the whole being the measurement of our individualism. The African poets, therefore, can only assume what their communities assume and not the other way round. I have written elsewhere that neither colonialism nor imperialism changed the face of African literature. Instead, it was the oral literature that found its way into the written text. Chinua Achebe's stories are the fireside stories of pre-colonial Africa, and Christopher Okigbo is a good example of an African poet who took after the myth of the oral charmers.

> Before you, Mother Idoto, naked I stand
> before your watery presence a prodigal
>
> leaning on an oilbean
> lost in your legend…

Whitman and Okigbo, quoted above, serve as appropriate examples of poet of private space and poet of public space respectively. Whitman's "Leaves of Grass" and Okigbo's "Idoto" are both canonic in their cultural domains. In composing their powerful openings, both establish a relationship between self and other. "Before you, Mother Idoto, naked I stand" is antithetical of Whitman's "I celebrate myself." Both poems are a celebration, in which Okigbo is recognizing a higher power to a point of agreeing to the concept of reductionism, and Whitman is expressing the individualism of the self to a point that everything without him suffers his deconstructionism. For Okigbo, the individual is only a part of a grander whole—the self is a part that requires the myth that acceptance is itself a source of life. At no time, therefore, could it be wise to imagine that a half (being the self) can detach from the whole. Whitman on the other hand knows of only the myth of growing, the myth of becoming, and the myth of detaching. There is no going back, no *prodigalism*. The two poets in their various ways are proving that the poet, wherever s/he may be, is not a myth maker, for to be a poet is itself a myth of articulation. Allan Grossman who believes that "power flows from knowledge of the prophecy" also believes that "the poetic maker is both the beneficiary and the judge of the logic of the practice." While Okigbo surrenders his individualism and becomes swallowed up by Idoto's legend, Whitman celebrates his independence. Let us entertain Michael Ryan's view of poets of 'primitive cultures' to appropriate Whitman and Okigbo and to appropriate African and Western poetry:

> Anthropology has shown us many cultures in which poets were "big shots." In primitive tribes, extant and extinct, the poet is usually the central figure, the Shaman-healer. Because he is close to the gods through his "divine madness," he keeps the tribe together by celebrating in his chants and sacred rituals its shared beliefs, ancestry, and cosmology. The tribe depends on the poet for its life.

Subsequently, Ryan states, "This may be too difficult for Rocky, or us, to understand, stuck as we are in the middle of a powerful industrial capitalist culture in which the primacy of self and the ostensibly inalienable rights of the individual are two essential elements of the encompassing myth." Ryan has made categorical statements regarding poets in 'primitive environments' that raise eyebrows. He has basically commented on the poet and the sacred, the poet and power, the poet and essence, and the poet and myth. In making a case for individualism in industrial capitalism, Ryan fails to capture community moments in the so-called primitive cultures. He singles out the poet and labels him a big shot, a dictator, a divine-healer, and a spiritual head.

From the jungles of the Apache (Ryan's backyard) to the heartland of Africa, no poet could be said to have performed in any of the offices into which Ryan relegated him or her. Unfortunately, Ryan did not provide evidence of any poet in primitive times being a "big shot," whatever that might mean. However, I assume that Ryan is confusing the poet with occultists and other spiritual perverts who engage in gross incantations. The rest of the other nomenclatures that Ryan argues that the poet falls under are not as well defined. As for his and Rocky's fear of losing their individualism (were these situations to obtain in their industrial capitalist culture), Ryan needs to be reminded that individualism is never entirely exclusive of collectivism, even in industrial capitalist cultures and vice versa. David Augsburger's astute observation specifies that the "so-called primitive societies often have . . . solutions that are more effective in bonding adversaries and blending goals than those groups who designate themselves as advanced, developed, or possessing far more data about human relations." The tribe in 'primitive cultures' did not depend on any one man for its survival, especially in Africa.

I am aware of the seemingly narrow Africa-versus-the-West position I have taken in an essay that promises to examine African poetry *vis-à-vis* the cultural forces in world poetry, which obviously should include Asian, Latin American, Caribbean, and Pacifican poetry. By this position it would also seem that I am assuming that Western poetry is the universal standard by which to examine all other kinds of poetry. Perhaps a reader who agrees with me that Western imperialism is omnipresent in all other political systems in the entire world will very soon see that Western poetry has partly been used as a vehicle to achieve that goal. Certainly, no two cultures hold the same view of poetry. For instance, I found this very interesting statement on one website:

> Western culture, which was influenced by

> Shakespeare, Milton, and the Romantic poets, had a pronounced tendency to think of poems as ornate, elaborate creations made by a few men of genius. Chinese culture, influenced by the anonymity of the *Shih Ching*, had a tendency to think of poems as something written by common humanity for the eyes of other humans.

Maybe that is where African and Western poetry separate and where African poetry also differs from its Chinese, or more broadly, its Asian counterpart. African poetry could possibly be imagined to fall between Western and Asian poetry. In Africa, after the Word of the poem is uttered, it becomes a community treasure. Very soon the poet goes into relative obscurity. The poet is a slave to the Word; therefore, it is not correct that the poet plays a power role in his community. Given the low-level socio-political position the *griot*-poet occupies in traditional Africa, African poets could be called "common humanity" endowed with the inspiration of the gods. The African traditional poet might not be a genius, but his or her society has "a pronounced tendency to think of his or her poems as "ornate, elaborate creations."

References

Aleshire, Joan. "Stay News: A Defense of the Lyric" in Poets Teaching Poets: Self and the World. Gregory Orr & Ellen

Bryant Voigt (eds). (The University of Michigan Press, 1996). p. 28.

Chinese Poetry http://web.cn.edu/kwheeler/chinese_poetry.html (retrieved 01/19/2006)

Rich, Adrienne. Blood, Bread, and Poetry: Selected Prose 1979-1985. (WW Norton & Company, New York, London, 1986). p. 108.

Simpson, Louis. The Character of the Poet. (The University of Michigan Press, 1986). p. 13.

Hallowell, Gbanabom. Drumbeats of War. (Author House, 2004). p.9.

Simpson, Louis. The Character of the Poet. (The University of Michigan Press, 1986). p. 8.

Soyinka, Wole. "Dedication." http://www.cs.berkeley.edu/-richie/poetry/html/aupoem45.html (retrieved 01/19/2006).

Mazrui, Ali. Cultural Forces in World Politics. (James Curry, Oxford, 1990). p. 94.

Larson, Charles. Under African Skies: Modern African Stories. (Farrar, Straus and Giroux, New York, 1999). p. xiii.

Nicol, Abioseh. "The Meaning of Africa." Personal papers of Davidson Sylvester Hector Willoughby Nicol (The author's official name).

Jackson, Richard. (2003). Unauthorized Autobiography: New and Selected Poems. (The Ashland Poetry Press, Ashland University, Ohio, 2003). p.16.

Joseph, George. "African Literature" in Understanding Contemporary Africa. April A. Gordon & Donald L. Gordon (eds). (Lynne Rienner Publishers, 2001). p. 332.

Nketia, J. H. "The Poetry of Drums" in From Black Africa. (ed) David Wells, et al. (Harcourt Brace Jovanovich, 1970). p.166.

Whitman, Walt. Leaves of Grass. (ed) Malcolm Cowley. (The Viking Press, New York, 1959).

Okigbo, Christopher. "Path of Thunder," 1968 (in the literary magazine Black Orpheus).

Grossman, Allan. "Orpheus/Philomela: Subjection and mystery in the founding stories of Poetic Production and in the Logic of our Practice" in Poets Teaching Poets: Self and the World. Gregory Orr & Ellen Bryant Voigt (eds). (The University of Michigan Press, 1996). p.121.

Ryan, Michael. "Poetry and Audience" in Poets Teaching Poets: Self and the World. Gregory Orr & Ellen Bryant Voigt (eds). (The University of Michigan Press, 1996). p.159.

Chapter 4

Scarification and Memory: A Review of Ahmed Koroma's *Of Flour and Tears*

Of the thirty poems in *Of Flour and Tears*, written by Ahmed Koroma, the first poem I read was "I Sit and Watch." I immediately asked myself why the persona in the poem sits and watch. Reading some more, I quickly discovered that the symbol of sitting and watching spans the entire collection. Of course, the poem contains a list of events the persona sits and watches: he sits and watches terror coming to reign for a long time, lions roaring at the resistance put up by tigers while pigs bow their heads in solitude after betraying the tigers. All of these actions seem to move the persona to sing a sad song.

In the entire collection, the persona is sitting and watching episodes in the jungle of his community. The act of sitting and watching these episodes is exactly what the entire mind is experiencing in the collection. Watchers, especially if they feel they have the responsibility to tell about what they watch, not only watch the activities, but also take them into their consciences through their moral pipes.

Ahmed Koroma, a new voice on Sierra Leone's poetic landscape is, all throughout the collection, in an obscure corner in a place he calls "Leo's Den," from where the episodes happening in his country bring to him sad songs. But he is not alone in the obscure corner. There are other helpless singers, who, more or less, form the choral dirge in this ensemble. "We clap our hands and sing sad songs/clad in frayed piece of woven cloth/battered but strong we will not fall/with worn-out zest we will stand tall" (p.51).

Koroma's "Leo's Den" is a mixture of lazy days and uneasy calm, where the lion feeds, the tiger resists with the fullness of its *tigritude*, and the pigs manufacture diseases. These are always a global caricature of orderliness in which every resident cashes a check: "Freetown's Wall Street merchants/trading tobacco and dollar bills/while we kick football/and play, sing and wish/for rain" (p.55).

There is too much rain in Koroma's collection. In fact, the opening poem is called "Rain." These are a multitude of reasons why any serious reader of Koroma's collection must treat that opening poem with all the momentousness it deserves. It is a wet poem, with everyone getting soaked by the drizzling clouds, the potholes, and the Akosombo dam. He even talks about the colors of water. Koroma chooses to identify only the red water that comes gushing from the dam, and this to me suggests that the dam itself has not benefited from human construction, and that it is in a very bad state of repair. Its dilapidated state can be perceived as a betrayal of the core. There are also many bridges, streams, contents soaking and rivers running, to the extent that one of the rivers even attempts an upward run.

It seems as if underneath this watery presence there is a Christopher Okigbo-like prodigal, lost in the legend of "The Red Sun." However, by way of departure, while Okigbo deifies Idoto, Koroma's persona is gripped by the raw fear of the red sun that "blinds those that dare to dream/those with zest and fervor, those unafraid to speak" (p.21). To the extent that the red sun is a terror in the life of the persona's community, even at night when the red sun is asleep, the community stays awake to "witness the red anopheles' flight" (.21). Effectively, the poet pushes the red card of human suffering under the ubiquitous red sun to include infesting with its malarial venom.

Koroma's Islamic faith features prominently in the collection. I have written elsewhere that the poet's songs are in accordance with the pulse of his or her community. Perhaps because Africa has had a history of survival, the communal has instilled in the African the sense of the whole being the measurement of our individualism. The African poet, therefore, can only assume what his or her community assumes and not the other way around. In Koroma's collection we see a fine blend of his two heritages: the ritualism of his African traditional customs and his Islamic legacy.

Usually, any collection of poetry will take its cover title from one of the poems in the book that manages to capture the sub themes of all of the other poems; however, Koroma has not followed that pattern. Instead, he focuses on the general theme of his collection and sees the need to grace his cover with a thematic title rather than one informed by the subject of only a single poem. This creative pattern results in a compelling experimentation. For instance, the portrayal of prayerfulness of people in his community and the acts of the mad man in the poem "The Mad Man" not only suggest an irrational and uncontrollable fit, but speaks to a common metaphor of the betrayal of the core.

To speak to the title of Koroma's collection, one must understand that Koroma's environment is a jungle where the fittest continuously prey on the weak; where the rest of mankind perpetually looks up to God to change automatically their misery to relief. The poem "Prayer" is the closest to the cover title of his collection. In the Eastern part of Freetown from where the poet hails, those of us who are residents of Freetown know that food sacrificial ceremonies are the order of the day. The act is locally referred to as *Sara*. In the poem "At the Wall," we witness critical mass in Kaibara City. All hopes that the system will rescue mankind are dying, thus the destructive resolve "death to democracy/we killed peace at last/lest it brings more peace/and democracy" (p.40). In this beleaguered state, divine intervention remains the only hope of the masses.

Koroma's collection represents two important elements: a ceremony for the dead taken away by the roughness of life and a ceremony to appease the divine to provide for the living.

Of Flour and Tears is at once the testimony of a young witness. It is a landscape of events in a time capsule of human misery. References to Western and African mythology neatly fuse with the original mind of the poet, thereby elevating the quality of the poems. To be considered a superior lyrical poet, one has to have a superior economy of expression. The poet's cautious use of expressions has protected the poems from losing their clarity and candor. Koroma demonstrates strong control over the three important elements in a poem: the opening, the enjambment, and the closure. He sustains mastery over these elements in all of his works. Whether he is writing in free verse or a mixture of free verse and the tightened forms, Koroma reveals his talent as a poet of images and symbols, and in the crafty use of metaphors to redefine his country's scarification and memory. Koroma is a delight to read.

References

Ahmed Koroma's Of Flour and Tears, a collection of poems (68 p.) Publish America (2012),Baltimore, MD, USA

CHAPTER 5

Pictures of Shame
A Review of Oumar Farouk Sesay's *Salute to the Remains of a Peasant*

When you read *Salute to the Remains of a Peasant*, do not congregate in your mind the four million peasants existing in Sierra Leone. Do not picture the remains of any peasant in the miserable lives of us the wretched survivors of our civil war. This volume is not about survivors. It is not about the living. It is not about the dead. It is not about you. It is not about me. It is not about the past. It is not about the present. It is not about the future. It is not about our hopes. It is not about our dreams. It is not about our mistakes. It is not about our achievements. It is not about our failures—all because it is not a book of blames nor is it a book of praise. This book is about a single peasant, whose remain lies within and between us.

In reading *Salute to the Remains of a Peasant*, I am guided by a philosophical theory known as "the veil of ignorance" as propounded by John Rawls in his book *A Theory of Justice*. Rawls argues, "'first of all, no one knows his place in society, his class position or social status" (p. 137). I allow myself to be led by a poet in his search for the cadaver of a peasant, one upon whose circumstance the greater circumstance could be understood, one upon whose demise is portrayed a fratricidal design Julius Caesar-like, with the poet pointing out and identifying the several swords of the nobility that murdered the lion of the Sierra. Oumar Farouk Sesay, in his several poems, shows me the remains of Caesar, the peasants' peasant, pointing to where the Brutuses, the Cassiuses, the Cascas, and all the other nobles stabbed the beloved lion.

Salute to the Remains of a Peasant is a collection of poems that focuses on a state of being. It is a work of still-life, the point at which our collective tension mangles and pauses forever! It is the artistry of the big bang, the theory of results. It is the physics of the elements of cause and effect. It is the geography of human features as created by our love, our anger, our temperament, our attitude, and our power. Along came a poet on life's pedestrian path. Oumar Farouk Sesay belongs to the generation of poets who happened on the road after the great mangling. Born in the 60s, Sesay did not witness the meanderings that eventually showed him the skewed image of the life of a peasant in Sierra Leone. What he came upon was "a thatched hut of mud/On the fringes of the forest/an unmarked heap of mud/In the depth of the forest."

Note the peasant world that took place in Sesay. Juxtapose the images of mud and 'forest." Also, juxtapose fringes, unmarked heap, and depth. When a poet shows great sensitivity to place like Sesay does, the reader is hooked. In these tight lines from the title poem, Sesay is whispering to his reader to tread cautiously on the temporality of the peasant so that before the thatched mud collapses, before the unmarked grave disappears, and before the forest closes in, someone, the unknown peasant whose "mortal mould of mud/Is laid to rest/After a life of unrest in the mud" is saluted.

Sesay is reliving the minds of Picasso and Goya and using the genre of poetry to expose the gothic and the obscure brought about by a bitter experience fashioned long before the decade of climatic rebellion that consumed the soul of Sierra Leone. The poet wants you to witness how, after Sierra Leoneans have been made in the image of God, the nobles of this country then re-manufactured them in the image of a peasant. Sesay is our own Dostoevsky.

Perhaps the question is what kind of a poet then is Oumar Farouk Sesay. In the literary world, there is always the tendency for critics to search from the list of older poets in order to understand the voice of a new poet. I defy that tradition for many reasons, but only one deserves to be mentioned here: Sesay, like many of us Sierra Leonean poets, comes from an obscure poetic background, not having been exposed to the country's literary tradition either in school or in his daily life. I shall, instead, determine what kind of poet Sesay is from a creative angle.

Sesay is a pacific as well as a tormented poet. It is rare to come across a poet with such an antithetical elemental combination. Sierra Leone does not have a dearth of pacific poets, with Gladys Casely-Hayford heading the list, or a dearth of tormented poets, with Syl Cheney-Coker heading that list. One may be tempted to insert Sesay as the mean between these two poets. But Sesay is not a mean, not in any Aristotelian sense.

Aristotle, in determining a mean, consented that two opposite extremes exist in human life. While Sesay in his poems does not quarrel with such a theory, he comes across as an unfolding, employing no more than the paintbrush of the fine artist as he lingers between several heavens and hells seeking the stillness of life in his country's pictures of shame. Sesay therefore, should be approached from multifaceted pole angles. Perhaps among Sesay's finest qualities, is his ability to compel anger while articulating reasoning. In the poem, "At Tellu Bongor," Sesay writes, "What prowls like hungry tiger in the Gola forest of my mind/ Is rage nursed to puncture your heart for raping your mother at/ Tellu Bongor" (p. 13).

Using the word peasant as a metaphor to lament his Sierra Leone, Sesay comes across to the fratricidal brother on a deeply moralistic note. The opening line cuts across like the chase of an eight hundred pound gorilla but in the second line the diction "nursed" softens the chase, with the prowling and hunger giving way to caution and strong dialogue. In pacifying his rapist brother and to help him see reason, the poet creates a dual metaphor of the peasant country: Tellu Bongor, the house of defilement and the greater country, and Sierra Leone the defiled.

In school, I was taught that the idiom, a thunderstorm in a teacup, is a hyperbole of reality, yet in Sesay's poetry of realism, a country can indeed be shamed in a teacup in a non-hyperbolic sense. Usually, many a great poem is destroyed by bad closures, and that is when the poet strays away from the thesis set in the opening lines. In "Tellu Bongor," Sesay's thesis is to reason with the fratricidal brother. It is gratifying to arrive with him at such a successful closure when he reminds the brother that "a hungry lion in the Kailahun of my mind is enraged/To snatch your galled heart at Tellu Bongor" (p. 13).

Remember that in his book, Sesay does not set out to alter the image of the remains of the peasant he writes about. His grand thesis, as I stated earlier, is to show a state of being. In reading Sesay, I am reminded of the work of a contemporary American poet, David St. John, who writes about his own work in an interview he gave to The Writer's Chronicle:

> I hope the colors act as a kind of musical/visual resonance that help to locate the reader, but I don't want to predetermine a particular scene or vignette. And I hoped the colors wouldn't limit the poem, so there could be degrees of red or green or blue, and the poems could be as soft and shifting as a prism of light on a wall.

I can picture Sesay articulating a similar concern about his poetry because *Salute to the Remains of a Peasant* has a rainbow of colors, a jamboree of musical instruments, and a choral ensemble. In "The Cry," he writes:

> The cry sucks strength
> From the gull of her despair
> Ebbs through the tides
> Strikes her vocal chords
> And explodes into the air
> Drenching the cacophony of groans (p.24)

In these lines, we are drawn to a galaxy of musical and visual images. At once the struggle to absorb in order to emit is seen through tight phrases, such as "gull, of her despair," "explodes," and "groans." Sesay is convinced that any experience as bad as the one in the lines above is capable of producing only a faulty tune, hence, "…the cacophony of groans."

While the pain and the struggle of this peasant produce disturbing music to the air, a technique the poet uses to articulate the true meaning of being a peasant, the poet, himself is a compelling lyricist, uses concrete and action verbs to convey music to our ears. In "He Did Not Die That Day" he writes, "When the tale of the toll/Of the war was told/In the warmth of our room/My husband folded the sleeves of his Ronko" (p.38). In "Driftwood," he writes, "The fading warmth of a feeble/Kiss is all I cling to" (p.82). In "Rebels," he writes, "A specter of Gloom/Loomed over the horizon/As zombies zoomed/The nation to doom/With the boom boom of bombs" (p.100).

Another of Sesay's compulsive nature is his superb referential ideology. In his seminal work, *Language and Self-transformation*, Peter Stromberg writes, "Behind a subject's language lies a set of events and emotions that the language transparently reflects" (p. 2). Indeed language is an essential agent of the poet's personality and, therefore, a fascinating experience.

Sesay writes about what I will call, the "peasantization" of Sierra Leone and our individual selves, but that is not all he intends. He also seeks to discover what one writer refers to as "the real self from the spurious self." Because the language and lyricism of Sesay's poetry reminds me of that of e.e. cummings, arguably America's greatest lyrical poet, I shall borrow from the words of Horace Gregory, a Cummings' critic, to appropriate Sesay, a poet who sustains an aphoristic language he has called his own, "a language of sharpened images and verbal wit and action—and mastered with great economy of phrasing."

As well as proving himself a master of closures, Sesay excels in enjambments, otherwise called line endings. Line endings require sound literary talent to construct a unique architectural poetry. In "The Child Who Danced" he writes,

> I was the Poster child
> Draped in rags
> Adorned with hunger
> Infested by pests
> Consumed by ignorance
> Who danced in celebration
> Of the new dawn (p.28)

Being a poet of practical sorrow, Sesay hangs his verbs on a rather transitive edge, so that the reader, gliding unto a succeeding plane of landscape in the next line is embraced by concrete nouns—suggesting that the poet is keener on realistic experiences than on surreal ones. And if a line ends with a noun, especially when that noun opens a sore in the heart, it often serves as an antecedent to succeeding lines of tactile images.

Among the poets of my generation, both within and without Sierra Leone, Oumar Farouk Sesay stands out as the most lyrical, reaching us more in sounds than in words. In this collection Sesay redefines the devices of onomatopoeia and assonance, poem after poem with new semantic flavor. The ten-year war of his Sierra Leone and that country's overall disastrous past serve as an accompanying instrument, helping him to dig deeper into the remnant of the life of the wretched and, indeed, into our collective and often abused humanity wherever. Reading Sesay's poetry is like witnessing the ebb and flow of the tide of human struggle in a past and present that will never again be a foreign country.

References

John, St. John. *The Writer's Chronicle*

Farouk Sesay's *Salute to the Remains of a Peasant*, a collection of poems published by Publish America: Baltimore, USA

Rawls, John. (1971). A *Theory of Justice*. Harvard University Press: Cambridge

Stromber, Peter. (1993). *Language and Self-Transformation: A study of the Christian Conversion Narrative* (Publications of the Society for Psychological Anthropology)

CHAPTER 6

A Fireside of Poems and Chants, a Phenomenological Review of *Contemporary Fireside Poems: An Anthology on Social Media* edited by Fatou Taqi and Philip Yamba Thulla

Motivated by the creative writing workshop amongst a group of members of the Sierra Leone Whatsapp Forum (SLWF), that led to the publication of the anthology *Contemporary Fireside Poems* (2016) edited by Fatou Taqi and Philip Yamba Thulla, this paper argues that the innovation brought about by social media can harness creativity amongst Sierra Leonean writers. While, over the years, Sierra Leone has lagged behind other countries in the sub-region in creative writing, social media has suddenly fired the imagination of writers and a dedicated commitment continues to manifest in the art. Globally, as well as locally, social networking for creative ingenuity is in its infancy state (Aragon et al, 2009; Ragbir & Mohan, 2012), but because its major characteristic involves "sharing and play among participants,"

(Aragon, et al, 2009) social media is contextually placed to enhance exploration, learning and discovery especially among young people (Bozkurt et al. 2016). Using the theory of phenomenological philosophy, I describe the task the social media writers' forum set for themselves—to produce their anthology and how their success can be considered an innovation in Sierra Leone.

Keywords: *Creative writing, innovation, social media; learning, poems, writers group*

In this paper, I provide a framework through phenomenological approach to understanding the extraordinary explosion of imagination and creativity in social media for creative writers. The approach examines a social media group experimentation that used their forum to produce an anthology of digital poems that was published as a hard copy in 2016. The use of social media to achieve a successful goal necessitated the study regarding media and how they influence human behavior. Hypothetically, the paper argues that the advent of social media has the capacity to heighten creative writing as well as creativity in all other disciplines, as well. In correlation, the paper postulates that with the innovation of the social media, creative writing in Sierra Leone has the tendency to sprout more prolifically currently than at any other time in the country's literary history. In a little over two months of announcing the anthology, the forum had poured over a hundred poems. In three months, the editors were inundated with so many submissions than they wanted for a single anthology. The question then becomes, what motivated these writers to amass quite an impressive body of work in a short time? With the phenomenological inquiry, I use a mixed-design descriptive approach to support the focus of this group experience to describe the event as fully and carefully as possible. The paper follows the process and the conversation on the forum, the social editing of the poems, and the rewriting of the pieces until the eventual publication of the anthology was achieved.

As a methodology of inquiry, phenomenological philosophy has been traced to Kant and Hegel; however, (Groenewald, 2004) the German philosopher, Edmond Husserl is widely credited for its development as a prominent research method of inquiry. The watch word in this philosophy is the expression "phenomenon." Bentz and Magilvy (2006, p.449) defined the phenomenological methodology as a way to "access the depth of personal experiences, as well as internally interpreted meanings of those experiences." Phenomenology is concerned about the innovation that emerges from personal experiences. The foundation of phenomenology is in the description of the phenomenon and an engagement with participants of the targeted event by way of interviews (Norlyk and Harder, 2010).

When we talk about social media, the images that come to mind are computers, phones and the Internet. Of recent times, the phone handset has almost replaced the computer. Many more phones are now capable of performing all of the functions of the computer. Mobile phones are handy and could be carried around as easily as one would carry money in one's pocket—because of that singular added advantage, phone handsets are largely preferred to computers. What then is social Media? Social media has been described as networking sites that allow individuals and groups of people to interact and share ideas and information in virtual communities. These sites have the capacity to network people regardless of where they are located in the real world.

The Making of the Anthology

About two years ago, I founded the Salone Writers' Forum on WhatsApp, and I invited many of the Sierra Leonean writers I had worked with in other circumstances. They, in turn, invited other writers they knew about, who themselves, invited other writers they knew about. Outstandingly, for the first time in my life, in a short period of time, I got to meet many more Sierra Leonean writers than I had ever known of in the twenty something years of my writing career by engaging with them via electronic media. Occasionally, one or more members discovered new writers, and were added to the community. Seasoned and budding writers in Sierra Leone finally found the community that brought them together.

Before long, the forum bubbled with vivacious creativity in the two main genres of poetry and fiction. The forum grew into a virtual workshop populated by Sierra Leonean writers at home and around the world, all with serious commitments in flourishing creativity, commentaries, reviews and editing, operating as the machinery of engagement at every tick of the clock. Creative writing via social media is a new phenomenon in Sierra Leone and members did not shy away from that fact. Even in global perspective, (Ragbir and Mohan, 2012) the consensus is that creative writing through technology is yet in its infancy.

As the accessories of the forum's human relationships fell into place, allowing for the new membership of virtual writers to feel more comfortable to open up their private spaces to the public forum, and, followed by the positive reactions of colleague writers, members became bolder and uploaded manuscripts of stories and poems from their phones. Nothing fires the imagination of any writer more than a timely and an encouraging feedback. The forum proved to be of immense support to the members. In the creative writing-through-digital environment to produce positive outcomes, Ragbir and Mohan (2012) noted that members "are required to imagine an idea or solution to a problem, create something, play with the creation in terms of improvements, changes etc., share it with others and reflect on what was done so that the next iteration can be improved or built upon." That was exactly what happened in the making of the anthology. Someone generated a thematic subject and everyone was asked to write a poem on it.

One remarkable accomplishment of *Contemporary Fireside Poems* is that, the product became a child of the Salone Writers

Forum, hence about a hundred people contributed to making it. Edited by Dr. Fatou Taqi of the Department of Language Studies, Fourah Bay College, University of Sierra Leone, and Mr. Philip Yamba Thulla of the Department of Literature in the Institute of Language Studies, Njala University, the anthology brought together the voices of twenty-five Sierra Leonean poets. Nine of the poets are female. The demographic appeal also attracted almost equal representations of age brackets of younger and older poets. More importantly was the diversity at play among the members. The personal and cultural highways and the cross-breeding of different values surfaced in the poems with the intensity of heat and cold and of ebb and tide. Whereas only twenty-five poets contributed to the anthology, at the time of the project, there were a hundred writers engaged in the cyber exchange process. The conversation leading up to the making of the anthology was overwhelming.

Contemporary Fireside Poems speaks to the testament of the efforts of the virtual relationship established on the Salone Writers' Forum. The research of Ragbir and Mohan (2012) accurately reflects on the drama that characterized the process of producing the anthology under review. The virtual workshop to put the book together was like a family affair that many of the members had not experienced before then. As a young writer, I visited a solitary and aged Sarif Easmon in his Victorian residence at Bathurst Street in Freetown, where he wrote his manuscripts on an archaic typewriter, and a decade later, I witnessed yet another solitary writer, Syl Cheney-Coker, punching his manuscripts of poems on the first computer I ever glossed my hand over.

You notice that I described both writers as being solitary writers. Anachronistically speaking, writing has always been perceived as an intensely personal affair. Therefore, it is astounding to say the anthology under review was an experimentation of a more 'public', albeit scientific, approach, to its compilation of spontaneously contributed submissions to the forum via mobile phones. What a striking achievement that the poems were composed on the phones of the writers, even so sporadically, usually in responses to uploaded poems that served the efforts of immediate inspirations. Unless one felt the heightened inspirational heat under which the anthology was assembling itself, one would not know the alacrity that came upon the writers who stayed up late nights around the clock to pour in new poems.

As the poems poured in, Professor Dr. Osman Sankoh (also known as Mallam O), who is a member of the forum and founder of the Sierra Leonean Writers Series, encouraged members to work toward publishing the hundreds of poems and stories pouring into the forum, as a book. From among the membership, the challenge brought to the fore two editors, equally new to the technology, who agreed to compile the digital stories and poems. They did a commendable job in bringing out the anthology under review. They are even working on another anthology dealing with short stories, expected to be published soon. Note that a major criterion for any of the forum members to be published in either anthology was that a work had to be first uploaded on the forum to allow as many comments and editing by the general membership before it was then taken away by the two editors for detailed final editing.

Structurally, *Contemporary Fireside Poems* is anthologized in authorial sequence rather than thematic, although much of the exercises that resulted in the book took a thematic approach in the virtual exchanges. There were themes such as abortion, love, travelogue, religion, philosophy and several mundane others. The aim of the book was not so much directed on the thematic structure, but on the artistry of the Sierra Leonean art. Regardless of the fact that several members anthologized in the book had made a name for themselves in the genre with notable publications, yet the central value of the collective whole demonstrate the metaphor of a wild escapade of Sierra Leonean traditional festival around bonfire. In other words, the anthology is an out-dooring of Sierra Leonean poets regardless of the poets' classifications, sophistications, longevity in the art or prolific standing.

Poetry comes on the page in different shapes and forms

depending on the perception of the poet, but there are two significant aspects of a poem the poet is concerned about while designing his or her lines: the enjambment: that is what constitutes a line in a poem, and, how lengthily the line is supposed to run and break off to lay over to the next line; then there is the concern about closure: that is, how the poet closes his or her thought process in the poem. However, focusing on the experience of the anthology under review, only the enjambment deserves to be discussed here. With regards to enjambment, there could appear some difficulties, if one were to compose a poem, of a line that is longer than the screen of a phone could allow, before the line lays over to the next line. During the exercise, there were no mentions made regarding the structures of each poem; however, after several comments made by forum members on the poems, the edited poems usually resurfaced on the forum in structures other than they had first been posted. Poets composing a poem on the phone and caring to maintain a deliberate enjambment would have to pay attention to the metrics of the lines. In the phone format, the line of a poem would have to mind the limits of the screen. Some of the poets only paid attention to line breaks when they had to send better edited copies of their poems in their preferred publication formats.

The writers who eventually got their poems to be included in *Contemporary Fireside Poems* spoke of how much they valued their experiences—all evident in their excitement of being published! What started as "sharing and play among participants" grew into a published national statement, a contribution to the literary growth of the nation of Sierra Leone, but even so, to the literary growth of the writers. Are there lessons to learn from this narration of the events that led to the publication of *Contemporary Fireside Poems: An Anthology*? How generic could this lesson be to the wider spectrum of other professional bodies in particular, and to educational institutions in general in Sierra Leone?

Social Media and Creative Innovation

Indeed, what the editors of the anthology have done can be described as creative and innovative. Such innovation can also be associated with other fields of human endeavor. Rothenberg & Hausman, (1976) noted that "creativity has direct pertinence to diverse types of disciplines and to the enhancement of humanistic goals in our technological and atomic age." We can talk about creativity and imagination in commerce, scientific undertakings, and politics.

A team of researchers (Bozkurt, Aydn, Taskirin, Koral, 2016) referred to the migration of creative writing from manual to digital as a "Renaissance." In their own words, Bozkurt, et al, (2016) noted that this renaissance has presented "a new kind of species called *Homo Iunctus*, who lives in a connected world and forms a superior connected being." However, they were careful to note that the being known as Homo Iunctus is superior only in terms of the sophistication of its technology that requires a paradigm shift for "affected generation whose perception of life is strongly related to digital technologies."

Based on this reality, the team, (Bozkurt et al. 2016) postulated that the process of creative writing on a digital level requires Homo Iunctus principles of exploration, discovery and learning. *Contemporary Fireside Poems* emerged from the level of engagement that combined exploration, discovery and learning. Initially, poets had to deal with the dichotomy of creativity, stepping from the private places to the public domain, then, that of struggling to compose poems on phone, and learning to better the process each posting.

To ensure that a writer benefits from digital creative writing such a writer has to be ready to explore the possibilities of the World Wide Web. Fortunately, there are many more writers exploring the Internet than are there stuck to the old model typewriter. According to my estimation, young people spend almost their entire lives spanning the virtual world. If the phrase, "catch 'em young" is anything to go by, and Sierra Leone being a majority youthful population, educational authorities would heighten the literary and academic standards of the country by channeling modes of learning mainly through the technology that encourages exploration and discovery. There has to be a way of addressing this concern through learning to ensure that individual participants as well as group networks succeed in their innovations. The desired outcome is to build favorable group attitudes. Contact theory shows that (Pettigrew & Tropp, 2006) in the initial stage there is always an organizational anxiety. "These feelings grow out of concerns about how they should act, how they might be perceived, and whether they will be accepted."

Learning can assume numerous forms. For example, a group therapy concept proposed by Muzafer Sheriff, a Turkish psychologist, (Johnson & Johnson, 2006) stated that projects should be fired by 'superordinate' goals. More than wanting to collaborate with someone with whom one has the same goal, one should wish to work with someone that has a burning desire to eradicate a certain problem. "The contact among members of different orientation needs to be structured so that attention is focused on a superordinate category that encompasses members in a social group" (Johnson & Johnson, p.428, 2006). In such environments, learning is sure to be the guiding force of collaboration and adaptation.

Contemporary Fireside Poems is a forceful case for social media in creative writing. Ragbir and Mohan (2012) argued that social media is structured for a more engaging form of learning, and that it encourages collaboration instead of cliques. In putting together *Contemporary Fireside Poems*, all members of the forum looked up to a process of engagement: first it were colleague writers who provided the initial feedbacks and then the editors took the manuscripts, worked with the individual poets, and polished them in readiness for publication. There remains no room for cliques in social media education, since education in that environment is one I refer to as "all put in all gain from." In quoting Graeme Harper, a leading scholar in this environment, Vanderslice (2016) noted that poets could be "the biggest winners in the digital world and the leaders in figuring out how to make digital projects part and parcel of the humanities." In the creative arts, poets are considered the most lucid of creators. They are able to twist images from mere thought processes to make them as attractive as they are accessible on the digital page. On the screen of a phone and a computer, poetry has become the sharp slice of knowledge to the quick young mind and a reminder of its brevity to the witty old mind.

A cursory look at the academic terrain in our schools and universities today shows that education in the humanities has plunged significantly from the pinnacle of engagement it enjoyed in the days grammar schools were grammar schools, and seems to be gagged by the binding wires of the rising spate of technology. Today our young minds prefer to watch cheap drama on the television page instead of reading compelling stories on the paper page; when they should be laying constructive arguments, and deploying their critical thinking on the paper page, they scavenge the Internet page to plagiarize from the wells of Google "knowledge." Having said that, no progressive academic or institution of academia can afford to distance itself from digital technology; however, it must be remembered that while the Internet technology has not come to rob from the scholastic superiority of the humanities nor undermine the valuable and compelling roses of creative writing from the abstract human talent, yet unless the human capacity appeals to one for the benefit of the other, both technology and creativity through the humanities will needlessly fall apart,

Ironically, while our young population deifies the inventions of mobile phones, iPads, iPods and their attendant software and social media itself, our educational institutions have refused to embrace these simple play-and-have-fun technologies into the school system. To do so both contextually as well culturally, would easily revive the humanities as a powerhouse discipline in our classrooms. I can only hope and pray that Taqi and Thulla continue to exploit social media for the benefits of their classrooms, and that their academic colleagues, if not already at it, would plunge in the endless depth of the World Wide Web to cause a seismic shift in their pedagogical approach to teaching and learning for the benefit of discovery and exploration!

Questionnaire to Participants

The following was the set of questions I posted on the Salone Writers Forum for all the members who participated in the making of the anthology. I then briefly summarized the responses of the participants.

> Was the digital poetry project by Taqi & Thulla the first time you participated as a group member in putting together the digital anthology for book publication?
>
> Did the experience of contributing to the group digital poetry project stimulate your imagination to write more poems?
>
> What positive effect did the exercise leave with you?
>
> Do you see yourself composing poems mostly now on your phone than it was before?
>
> Are you looking forward to more of these exercises?
>
> Have you transferred your experience to other disciplines of your interest?

During the preparation of this paper, I posted the above questionnaire to the forum and the writers responded to them. The questions were meant to attract members who submitted as well as those who did not submit poems, but were participants in discussing the poems on the forum. The overwhelming majority of the respondents confessed it was their first time they were participating in putting the digital book together; they also responded that the exercise increased their writing productivity. All sides of the demographic divide responded that it was fun writing poems on their phones, and that the exercise had become part of their daily routine. They also responded that they were looking forward to future exercises; and that they had begun a discussion of their other interests using social media.

Summary Questionnaire to the Coeditors

I asked both editors to describe the fulfillment they received in editing the anthology: Dr. Fatou Taqi responded that the fulfillment she had was in working with a partner, team member, co-editor, with two different perspectives and how they agreed to disagree while compiling the anthology. For his own part, Philip Thulla noted that coediting the anthology was a fulfilling experience. He acknowledged that it was his first time engaging in professional editing; however, he felt that working with a more experienced coeditor triggered for him, a new experience. He noted that the exchanges with writers and his coeditor presented a real lifetime learning endeavor for him.

I also wanted to know what hope they saw for digital creative writing in Sierra Leone in the social media age. Dr. Taqi said she saw hope only if there would be a cost effective reliable Internet service to ensure a truly effective sharing of soft copies of manuscripts among writers. Mr. Thulla responded that with the decline in the reading of the printed page, social media, he said had a great promise for growth. He added that with social media creative writing, there would be a better opportunity for mentorship, coaching, and that even the market could expand for social media creations.

Conclusion

Innovation has been the central concern of this paper. The study tried to show how a Whatsapp group of a hundred Sierra Leonean writers, many of whom were only newly exposed to digital creative writing, willingly explored, discovered, and learned the technology that could make them better as well as more committed writers. The climax of the project, being the printing of a hard copy of the anthology of twenty-five poets was what attracted the use of the phenomenological approach to the study. The study also solicited responses from the participants of the project who responded overwhelmingly to the positive impression the project left on them. Based on this study, it is the opinion of the author of this paper that, be it creative or academic education, a better attractive form of engagement among young people would be to enhance technology at the center of it. As per my research question on what motivated the members of the forum to amass quite a body of work in the short time they set to putting an anthology together, I found out the following: social media contributed immensely in helping members become more productive; members developed superior sense of critiquing each other's works; and members produced better quality of poems as compared to when writers of yore treated the art of writing as an intensely private matter with only a singular story to their inspirations.

References

Aragon, C.R., Poon, S.S., & Aragon, D. (2009). "A tale of two online communities: Fostering collaboration, and creativity in scientists and children." ACM conference on Creativity and cognition.

Bentz, K. N., & Magilvy, J. K. (2006). When a partner dies: Lesbian widows. *Issues in Mental Health Nursing*, 27(5), 447-459.

Bozkurt, A., Aydin, B., Taskiran, A., Koral, E., (2016). Improving creative writing skills of EFL learners through microblogging. *The Online Journal of New Horizons in Education*. Vol. 6, Issue 3.

Groenewald, T. (2004). A phenomenological research design illustrated. *International Journal of Qulaitative Methods*. 3 (1) April.

Johnson, D.W & Frank P. Johnson. (2006). *Joining together: Group theory and group skills*, 10th edition, Pearson: Upper Saddle.

Norlyk, A., Harder, I., (2010). What makes a phenomenological study phenomenological? An analysis of peer-reviewed empirical nursing studies. *Qualitative Health Research* 20(3) 420-431

Pettigrew, T.F. & Linda R. Tropp. (2006). "A meta-analytic test of intergroup contact theory" in *Journal of Personality and Social Psychology* 2006, Vol.90.No.5.751-783.

Ragbir, D., Mohan, P., (2012). *Using Social Networking Technologies to Harness Creativity amongst Students*.
https://pdfs.semanticscholar.org (Retrieved March 10, 2017).

Rothenberg, A., & C.A. Hausman, (ed). (1976). *The Creativity Question*. Duke University Press: Durham.

Salone Writers Forum. (2017). Interviews with members of the forum on their experiences in writing digital poetry, leading up to the publication of *Contemporary Fireside Poems: An Anthology*. SLWS 2016.

Taqi, F., Thullah, P.Y. (2017). Interview responses on the publication of their book they edited, Contemporary Fireside Poems: An Anthology.

Vanderslice, S., (2016). Beyond the Tipping Point: Creative writing Comes of Age. *College English*. Vol. 78, No. 6.

PART II
ON CULTURAL VALUES

CHAPTER 7

Feeding, Eating and the Politics of Food

> Keynote address delivered at the Scaling up nutrition end of year strategic food and nutrition security coordination meeting held Thursday December 10, 2015 at the Office of the Vice President of Sierra Leone

---

Bread
by Syl Cheney-Coker

The spoon was walking, full, off the table
to reach the poor and all their Sundays,
all their lost mornings came rushing back
hungry as the lion's eyes; the table was moving
toward the centre, breaking its legs
and all their journeys came inward to their stomachs
reeking of this great forest's hunger
the loaf was walking out of the oven announcing
its magic yeast and the mouths of the poor
began to shake trying to catch the taste of its smoke

As someone without any background in nutritional studies, academically speaking, I cannot think of any possible reason I have been asked to deliver this keynote address other than that the organizers probably suspected that for as long as Gbanabom Hallowell lives he craves to be fed, he will have to eat, and that he will constantly be engaged in the daily politics of food. I just turned fifty years November 27, only four years younger than independent Sierra Leone. For fifty years Sierra Leone has fed me, and in turn, I have been engaged in the business of eating and in the politics of food. By my emphasis on this matter you have probably realized that there are three processes involved in the feeding-eating arrangement in the life of a single individual, a single family, a single community and a single country.

The Verb to Feed

This delivery will understand feeding to mean man's ability to secure food, a family's ability to put food on the table, a community's ability to protect food ration, and a Government's ability to sustain food supplies. Feeding is not only a constant must but a political enterprise that requires a creative commitment. The verb to feed is not similar to the verb to eat. Like all verbs, both of them require ability; however, the ability to feed is different from the ability to eat. The process of feeding begins with the acceptance, at the levels of the individual, the family, the community, and the Government, that feeding can only occur where the act is considered a responsibility of one unit to another: of the Government to the community, of the community to the family, and of the family to the individual. In agrarian times, it was difficult for communities to constitute because man primarily lived and wrestled in the wild of the jungle and the vastness of the sea. As such, he was constantly migrating from place to place for as long as the seasons brought forth food or famine. In modern society the responsibility of feeding a nation that must remain firmly rooted in its base requires the responsible unit to encourage productivity, preservation and banking. The Economist, Paul Collier, in an article in *Foreign Affairs* noted that "Feeding the world will involve... politically challenging steps. First, the world needs more commercial agriculture, not less. Second, the world needs more science."

In Sierra Leone, the key player that comes to mind in the promotion of commercial agriculture and more science is the Ministry of Agriculture. I grew up as a child at a period Annual Agricultural Shows where held in almost every major district headquarter towns. These shows were meant to educate and inform the nation how the governments, donors and farmers were developing increased technology and scientific techniques in crop production and animal husbandry. I have not witnessed such a display for a long time, but my hope is that such a practice continues in pockets of congregations of producers, distributors and consumers.

The Verb to Eat

I will understand eating to mean man's ability to consume, the family's ability to diversify food to eat, the community's ability to environmentalize food to eat, and the Government's ability to enhance the production of food to eat. Colleen Steelquist noted that "Eating is one of the more complex of human behaviors. We make a myriad of choices—or have little choice—based on values, availability, income, mood, taste, hunger and such." Growing up, and endlessly being forced to bury my head over the then popular *Student's Companion*, I have forever fished out my head from that timeless book with an expression known as *pantaphogist*, meaning, someone who eats all kinds of food. Well, it may be easy to cater for any such kind individual; but when one has to manage consumers whose eating habits are guided by values, income, availability, mood, taste and hunger as pointed out by Steelquist, it requires the setting up of movements such as Scaling Up Nutrition (SUN) to further support the efforts of organizations such as WFP, UNHCR and others who in turn support the efforts of the government, the community and the family. In the limited resources that there are, there are bound to be clashes of interests between those whose eating values are guided by religion and those whose eating values are guided by culture.

The irony of food is that it builds us and breaks us instantly or at a later time. Food can determine our intelligence, our ability and readiness to learn, our sexual potency, and our response to the natural habitat. Scientists have been able to determine that the longevity in age of most people on the Japanese Okinawa Island can be attributed to their eating habit. One website wrote about the Okinawa Islanders that "The secret of their highest life expectancy is because of their incredible knowledge of nutritional facts and eating techniques of the food items available around them. People from this tiny Japanese island consume nutrient rich, low-calorie diet (a diet averaging not more than one calorie/g) that is composed of low fat, less sugar, and sufficient in protein (available through small quantity of fish) but lots of green/orange/yellow (GOY) vegetables, and fruits."

The Ethics of Feeding and Eating

There is what is referred to as a feeding culture and an eating culture. These two cultures, both in their morphological features and in their relationships with each other, are dynamic. Many factors are responsible for their dynamism, but only two deserves to be mentioned here. The totality of these factors can best be discussed in detail in another engagement. Two factors that necessitate the dynamism of these cultures are the biological and ecological changes that man and his environment constantly experience. As I deliver this paper, world leaders are grappling with the environmental degradation threatening to annihilate photosynthetic life on earth. While, in its totality, the threat may not materialize in our lifetime, yet the gradual hell-push is beginning to rear its head in the poor quality of food we eat.

Ethics plays a significant role between the hand that feeds and the hand that eats. Between feeding and eating lies the required element of altruism. In a normal situation, we stand to achieve little if we only provide food for the sake of providing food that someone can get fed. We equally would be achieving little substantial if we keep eating the wrong food. It is unfair to think that the hand that feeds is superior to the hand that eats. Rather, in many respects the hand that feeds serves as an eating instructor. Through what the feeding hand produces, the eating hand survives. The child comes into this world with no knowledge of what to eat to grow well, yet ahead of that child's arrival, the feeding hand exists and knows what to provide. Charlotte Biltekoff argued that "…to eat right could create responsible citizens and address problems in the social order—from nihilism to violence and environmental degradation."

I first heard the expression in Themne from an older cousin of mine regarding man's existence on earth, that *s'dae gbo karr ka di*, literally meaning "we are just here to eat" or "we are just here waiting to be fed" or "we live to eat and eat to live." It's a rather hopeless expression whose metaphor speaks to the vanity associated with the life of an individual—a reality that has the tendency to develop in some people a rather casual commitment to quality food. However, while as individuals we all expire in the end, yet humanity is not terminated. You have heard it said in a popular Christmas lyric that, "Man will leave forever more because of Christmas day." Nutritionally speaking, we can borrow from that leaf to say "Man will live forever more because of food."

If this statement is true, (noting that since the year zero human beings have grown to number seven billion without any break in the chain of human births), food, like shelter and clothing does not only exist to feed us, but to beautify and to make us civilize beings. The science of feeding and eating hold the key to sound socio-economic activity and development. The process of feeding and eating is based on the Hippocratic ethical code of beneficence, which means do good, and on the ethical code of non-maleficience, which means do no harm. Whether food for consumption is from commercial or philanthropic source, the onus is on the provider, through quality control measures, to ascertain that such food is not only good for consumption but has no possibility of causing any harm to the person who eats it, unless of course the latter chooses to abuse the principles of eating.

The Politics of Food

Dr. Roni Neff works at the John Hopkins Center for a Livable Future. She defined the food system as "everything it takes to produce and process food, advertise and bring it to customers, prepare it, and dispose of it. This includes the people and businesses involved, and the places, processes, policies, and politics that shape the whole system." Such a definition establishes the picture of a complex arrangement, a complex undertaking, and a complex relationship amongst all players of the food chain. We are talking here about food in the global sense of the word and in a global community whose proverbial pot has not always melted in the sense the United Nations has always wanted it to melt. But even when we bring the concept closer home to include the Government, the community, the family and the individual, the pot has not always melted as well as we describe it in our manifestoes, implement it in our communities and serve it in our families.

While my intention is not to paint a gloomy picture of the food system through and through, I think we would need to define my use of the expression "politics" as it relates to food. Against the background of a rich and a poor man left in the jungle to die of starvation, and, suddenly, there appears on sight the carcass of the leg of a dear devoured by lions, but a leg not even enough for either of the two men to eat to avoid death by hunger, greed, with all its egoistic tendencies provokes their selfish hormones. Such a situation no longer tastes of any human elements—it suddenly turns into the survival of the fittest.

The example I have just given guides my definition of politics in this delivery. Politics is here defined as the imaginary line between altruism and egoism in the management of the food system. From the manufacturing of food to its consumption, everything can go right and everything can go wrong. In 2014 Mike Adams, an American naturalist nutritionist and consumer activist alarmed the world when he asserted that "Based on what I am seeing via atomic spectroscopy analysis of all the dietary substances people are consuming on a daily basis, I must now announce that the battle for humanity is nearly lost. The food supply appears to be intentionally designed to end human life rather than nourish it."

Paul Collier warned that "in the developing world, a food shock of (any) magnitude is a major political event." Professor Kamari Maxine Clarke, an anthropologist argued that "violence in Africa begins with greed." We can now begin to appreciate the popular expression of food being a political commodity, perhaps the most important political commodity especially in developing countries. I think one of government's most successful programs in the direction of good feeding is its 'food for work' engagement programs. Such a program speaks directly to the heart of our youthful population.

The assertion made by Mike Adams is very disturbing. Please allow me to quote him at length here, and you decide whether what he has to say about the negative effects of bad food fed the world, also rings true about the effects of food consumption in Sierra Leone:

> This goes far beyond the mere contamination of foods with heavy metals -- a subject which is grave all by itself. Rather, this is about the intentional *formulation* of toxic substances into products consumed by the masses on a regular basis.
>
> The result is what you see unfolding around you right now: mass insanity, incredible escalations of criminality among political operatives, clinical insanity among an increasing number of mainstream media writers and reporters, widespread infertility in young couples, skyrocketing rates of kidney failure and dialysis patients, plus a near total loss of rational thinking among the voting masses.

> The effects of this are devastating to human civilization: the collapse of a capable workforce, the rise of the masses dependent on government for survival, the collapse of free democracies due to the cognitive retardation of the voting masses, an exploding prison population…

While some of the images in Adams' alarm may be locally contextualized, we are yet to experience some of the others. However, if we agree that these things happen in some other parts of the world, how can we doubt that they are capable of happening in our backyards? A cousin of mine and I were traveling from the provinces, and at a place called Limba Corner, we stopped to have a cup or two of palm wine. My cousin was not so sure the wine tasted well after he had gulped a first cup, and he did not hide his feelings:

"This wine is not good, it tastes like the leftover of the previous night," he said to the wine tapper.

"What do you mean, this is the wine the white people drink each time they pass by," the tapper protested.

"What?" My cousin exclaimed. Do white people know anything about the taste of good palm wine more than I do?"

When we talk about the politics of food we mean that as a government, a community, a family, and as individuals, we must make tough decisions to be in control of food commodities entering our borders and our bodies. We should not just leave all the conclusions in the hands of our bilateral and multilateral partners—we should empower our local institutions and experts to have the last word on all food items, deny any when it must be denied and accept any when it must be accepted. Food comes in solid and in liquid forms—for good or for bad they compete with homegrown food commodities. Their supplies, preservations and banking pose political challenges to the government, the community, the family and the individual. Supplied unfairly food distribution could provoke a crisis, preserved poorly, its conservation could provoke ill-health, banked in dilapidated places, its reservoir could result to insecurity.

Food Management in Post Ebola Sierra Leone

In the wake of the Ebola epidemic in Sierra Leone, citizens were shocked to learn that there was no known cure for the disease. Doctors began warning that the only way to conquer the disease was, in addition to the symptomatic drugs administered, patients must be ready to eat well to muster the needed energy to combat the disease. But for many Sierra Leoneans, especially those in the lower income bracket, the scare of the disease and the occasional restrictions of human movements created a catch-22 situation. Food did not only become scarce, even the little that was available did not always make a healthy diet. In a situation like this, Clemens Breisinger, et al noted that, "As a result, economies often contract, instability and insecurity spill over national borders, and food and nutrition insecurity rises."

Taking an introspective view of the combative measures marshaled to fight against Ebola, I begin to wonder whether anyone of us ever thought about the pivotal role nutritionists and other food experts could have played in the feeding and eating habits of the citizens at a time when food donations where eking from all over the country and from all over the world. Or for that matter, what if there were scrupulous business people who had large stocks of expired and damaged food commodities who found an opportunity in that chaotic moment to dispose of their bad food at cash value to unsuspecting citizens? Imagine that a sizeable number of these business people succeeded in releasing their stocks to the buying public, several months or years later, what imminent dangers await those of us who had consumed these foods in the thick of the Ebola crisis?

Food management in post-crisis could very well be as herculean a task as in inter-crisis. In the regions that were made vulnerable by poor borders and poor food supplies in pre-Ebola, there need to be a deliberate attempt at heightening authoritative government protection. The stories put forward regarding the first Ebola patient in Sierra Leone confused the real nationality of the victim, other than that he freely went back and forth from Sierra Leone to Guinea to family members on both sides of the border. Thousands of Sierra Leoneans go through porous borders on a daily basis across to Guinea and Liberia, with food substances serving as the major commodities returning into the country. It would be helpful to put a robust system in place to vet the quality of food migration.

Syl Cheney-Coker's poem, "Bread" the first stanza of which I opened with ended with "…the loaf was walking out of the oven announcing/its magic yeast and the mouth of the poor/ began to shake trying to catch the taste of its smoke." For the purpose of this meeting, I will extend the metaphor of 'poor' in Cheney-Coker's poem to include all of us who are 'innocent' consumers of food in the sense that we go to the market, or are given food whose production, preservation and banking techniques we do not care to, or do not have the time to enquire about. As hungry people, it is the instant that matters to us—the loaf of bread, hot from the oven should quickly find its way to our shaking mouths to save us from dying. Therefore as we are always fed in haste, and we eat in haste, our trust that we are fed and we eat quality food is reposed on the government, the community and the family to which we all belong—hence we are each other's keepers!

References

Adams, M. (2014). "Battle for humanity nearly lost: global food supply deliberately engineered to end life, not nourish it." *Natural News*, February.

Biltekoff, C. (2013). "Eat right here: The cultural politics of ethical eating". Utne Reader, December 2013.

Brescinger, C, et al. (2014-2015). "Conflict and food insecurity: How do we break the links?" 2014-2015 *Global Food Policy* report.

Clarke, K.M., (2013). "Treat greed in Africa as a war crime." *The New York Times*, January 2013

Collier, P. (2008). "The politics of hunger: How illusion and greed fan the food crisis". *Foreign Affairs*. November/December Issue.

Neff, R. (2009). "Food matters: How what we eat affects our health and the planet." Imagine, January/February

"Power your diet. Your guide to healthier nutrition." Welcome to nutrition facts in the food. http://www.nutrition-and- you.com/ (Retrieved Thursday December 4, 2015)

Steelquist, C. (2011). "The science behind what we eat." *Quest Online*. Summer 2011

CHAPTER 8
Upholding Ethical Values as Corruption Prevention Measures

> A paper delivered at the Ethics and Integrity Workshop for MDAs Organized by the Anti-Corruption Commission (ACC) at Santano House, Howe Street, Freetown at 9:30 a.m. Friday December 15, 2017.

Social, cultural, and religious morality continue to be relevant to the fight against corruption, particularly because they appeal strongly to the spiritual consciences of Sierra Leoneans, yet as learned from the social sciences, the upholding of ethical values, which mainly advocate altruistic and utilitarian behaviors over egoism, toward the welfare of others, can serve as an efficient corruption prevention measure in civil and public office..

In their invitation to me to deliver a paper on "Upholding Ethical Values as Corruption Prevention Measure," the Anti-Corruption Commission (ACC) informed me that their invitees are entirely civil servants from different Ministries, Departments, and Agencies (MDAs). True to their word, delegates have all come from the MDAs. Listening to the mention of the three bodies above, anyone unfamiliar with the official arrangements of these establishments may be tempted to think that these establishments are three mutually-exclusive bodies of invitees. That assessment may be so; it may be not.

In the matter of managing government and country, the hierarchy of authority begins with the political figures who belong to the governing class, then the civil servants who are the custodians of the nation's assets and wealth, the agencies that provide specialized public services complimentary to the earlier two, and then, subsequently, the military, which is the security power house of the nation's assets, wealth, and human resources. The establishments are certainly not mutually exclusive.

I may not be a government civil servant, but I work in public broadcasting. Whereas all civil servants are public servants, not all public servants are civil servants. However, the paper I've been asked to deliver here is as relevant to me as a public servant as it is to the civil servant. Therefore, I look forward to benefiting from the deliberations of this meeting. I mention this as a benefit because as a public servant, I am held by the same standards to which the civil servant is held.

As civil and public servants, we have a responsibility to be mindful of how we conduct ourselves in government, as well as in public, for we are held in the trust of citizens and taxpayers. In regard to such a reminder, we are here today to examine how to uphold ethical values as corruption prevention measure in our various establishments.

The Face of Corruption

I was unable to find a satisfactory definition of corruption anywhere. As well, I was unable to develop any that would satisfy me. I, therefore, decided to associate words with the phrases "corruption" and "corrupt practices" to help me imagine a broader understanding of the concept and practice of corruption. You may have heard it said that corruption occurs every minute and not just in transitioning or developing countries. Corruption has become a global pandemic, at times even rearing its head in the western world, such as in the Breton Woods Institutions, in the UN agencies, and in other bilateral and multilateral economies of affluence, and sowing its gelatinous roots in Africa and other downtrodden regions.

As the issue of corruption becomes more and more complex and subject to all kinds of debates, it is important that we distinguish between a corrupt act and other unjust behaviors, for it is wrong to think of corruption as an act of revenge against any other act of injustice. In other words, a corrupt practice could never be defensible as a weapon against an act of a previous corruption or, for that matter, any kind of injustice done to anyone, community, or nation state. Therefore, an act of corruption is an absolute injustice, and as Heinze (p.48) rightly noted, "Some *acts* can only be seen as categorically unjust, that is, as unjust under *any defensible* ethics."

Of Morality and Corruption

Academically speaking, before corruption became a scholarly concern of the social sciences, it was unilaterally considered a moral wrong that was left in the domain of religion ahead of any legal consequences. Scholars and practitioners have not only broadened the focus on the fight against corruption, but also have questioned the dominant roles of morality and religion over ethics in the fight against corruption. In addition to the three domains I have mentioned, there is now the all-to- prominent ethics domain that points to a social scientific approach to the fight against corruption.

The fight against corruption has accommodated wider latitude of academic and practitioner interests addressing its ills. There now appears to be a democratic consensus among anti-corruption crusaders as to which domain addresses which corrupt practices and at what pace any such address might evolve before it assumes a scope and compass that would determine it to migrate from one level to another. Together, the four domains of morality, religion, legality, and ethics have come to constitute the ubiquitous weapon meant for the fight against corruption. According to the scholar, Lopez-Carlos (2014), "This means that in the long-term perspective, anticorruption strategies have to be supported by moral education and the strengthening of the ethical principles underpinning society" (p.1).

We must bear in mind that Lopez-Carlos is proposing a two-domain approach as a corruption prevention measure: moral education and the strengthening of the ethical principles that have now become the bedrock of the country's democracy. Certainly, because of the pivotal role religion plays in the lives of Sierra Leoneans, it is expected that religious values of right over wrong behaviors remain paramount to the salvation of adherents of the faiths. The expectation is that, when they die, in the context of exhibiting greed and desire for material wealth of the all too tentative mundane things or exhibiting spiritual trust for the things hoped for in heaven. As Lopez-Carlos noted again, "it may require institutions of government to support secular civic education. Religious leaders should move beyond their religious differences and focus on their primary function of leading the people to identify with their spiritual nature" (p.1)

Was there any reason for the fight against corruption to be salvaged from the total possession of religion, spreading it beyond the dimensions of morality? Writing in the tone of a moralist, Carlos-Lopez called for the moral self-examination of the religious leaders. He argued, "This may mean reinforcing the civic responsibility component of secular education. It may require religious leaders—who bear such heavy responsibility for the decline of religion as a force for social cohesion—to set aside narrow doctrinal differences and return to the spiritual roots of their respective faiths to revitalize their ability to lead individuals and societies to a stronger identification with the spiritual rather than the material dimension of human nature" (p.4)

In the case of corruption, legal intervention often results in an accused person's blemish of character, to punishment and damage of integrity if found guilty. The religious and moral dimensions are not known to employ any scientific or democratic methods to address acts of corruption other than an invocation of the wrath of God. Genocidal acts of corruption, perpetrated in history and today benefiting governments and economies in Europe and America and carried out through slavery and other economic tortures, have, over the years been only atoned for or against in the houses of God, while the ancestors of those who suffered the crucibles continue to live in chronic persistent poverty and psychological pain.

Cases, such as the Transatlantic Slave Trade, the extermination of the Jewish by the Nazis of Germany, the Japanese bombing of the Americans at Pearle Harbor, the dropping of bombs on the Japanese of Hiroshima by the Americans, the Rwandan Genocide between the Hutus and the Tutsis, and closer home, the slaughtering of innocent Sierra Leoneans between the government and Revolutionary United Force (RUF) or any act of human degradation that facilitated rogue governance and rogue economic gains, remain acts of corruption by a few against the so many and big scars on the skins of human history.

The term morality has become so elusive that it can no longer be singlehandedly relied upon to present a measure that will prevent the occurrence of corruption. Bear in mind that I am using the term morality loosely in the context of its religious, cultural, and anthropological pairing. In fact, there are three major categories of morality whose interpretations of the world we live in have provided challenges as to how to administer moral reasoning to persons of different moral orientations: the moral category, the immoral category, and the amoral category. There are those who are moral, and they are those who hold on to intrinsic rules into which they are born and bred. There are others, who are immoral, and they are those who deliberately disregard any moral rules of existence, and there are those who are amoral, those whose lives are not characterized by any moral values.

The possibility that these three categories of people can subscribe to common values as prevention corruption measure remains almost unachievable. Therefore, that ultimately leaves us with only one option: viewing corruption and the fight against corruption through an ethical lens. According to Carlos-Lopez there could only be one problem to deal with regarding this issue. He wrote, "Despite this, there is little in the literature on corruption to suggest that a moral framework is appropriate to analysis – yet this may be due to the nature of ethics itself. Ethics approaches moral dilemmas from several angles, which means that there never will be one single or definitive framework for the moral analysis of corruption" (p.2).

Of Ethical Values and Corruption

"What is ethics?" McNamara asked. "Simply put, ethics involves learning what is right or wrong, and then doing the right thing, but "the right thing" is not nearly as straightforward as conveyed in a great deal of business ethics literature. Most ethical dilemmas in the workplace are not simply a matter of "Should Bob steal from Jack?" or "Should Jack lie to his boss? (p.1)"

Upholding ethical values as a corruption prevention measure requires MDAs to institute what White refers to as "definable subsystems known as stakeholder groups" (p.1). Civil servants and public servants become aware of their selfless duty to serve humanity rather than to gratify their individual egos. In this respect, serving the community means engaging all stakeholders at critical levels for the benefit of all. The stakeholder groups are employees, customers, suppliers, financiers, and local communities.

What is required to move the dynamics around is ethical and creative leadership. Many institutions headed by dictators have, for instance, refused to open up to the views of women who want to conduct their business affairs without the value of any myths and ancient beliefs. The principle of ethical leadership states that there should be a respect of the views of others. Ethical leaders serve others, ethical leaders are just, ethical leaders are honest, and ethical leaders build communities. But by restraining one or the other group of people from participating in free economic activities or as in the case of the girl-child, from attaining the requisite education that can make them contribute to their community, the leadership would have acted unethical and corrupt.

Schwenke (2010) calls for an examination of ethnic loyalties and public loyalties in an environment where the common dogma, as he quoted a Kenyan mantra, has become, "It is our turn to eat." The scenario makes for an important addition to our subject. I certainly would not consider it a causal act of corruption. I would say that it is the effect of corruption that is capable of contributing to conflicts in countries at the brink of national civil strife.

Given the categories of stakeholders listed above, there are three different approaches to making decisions regarding ethical values:

Ethical egoism states that a person should act so as to create the greatest good for him or herself. For example, people picking up a job merely for their satisfaction. Self-interest is an ethical stance similar to transactional leadership. Egoism is also applicable to businesses purely concerned with profit-making (Maximizing profit).

Utilitarianism states that we should behave so as to create the greatest good for the greatest number. The morally correct thing is maximizing social benefits while maximizing social cost.

Altruism is an approach that suggests actions are moral if their primary purpose is to promote the best interest of others. Authentic transformational leadership is based on altruism.

In economically wretched societies, citizens usually find it difficult to speak truth to leadership regarding corruption. Such a culture underscores why, according to Schwenke (2013), a Ugandan minister, after prosecution, could walk the streets of Kampala, boasting, "It is our turn to eat." I think statehood and corruption require another level of discussion, perhaps never before addressed. This new attempt certainly has to go beyond or even help to rewrite Max Weber's concept of state politics, taking into consideration the unavoidable and forceful role of the global community in local governance, especially in the developing world. When governments and their people lose confidence in each other's integrity, it is usually the international community that becomes the judge. To an extent that peripheral states no longer possess the political strength, Max Weber talked about when he wrote, "A state is a human community that successfully claims the monopoly of the legitimate use of physical force within a given territory" (p. 1). No state survives for a day if its monopoly on legitimate violence is challenged by groups of rebellious people.

When states are at the brink of collapse, the international community becomes their gatekeepers. Where the international community, mainly the donors, holds a different view of corruption than those countries on the brink they undertake to salvage, a conflict is sure to ensue. To conceptualize the theories of corruption with strong global elements we could borrow from Couto (2013) who points us to the many studies of political environments, political leadership, structures, and processes to gain a deep "insight into how well particular leaders bent those structures and processes to their purposes or were bent by them" (p. 1). Examples abound of countries, such as Iraq, Libya, and Argentina, where, after it became apparent that their political leaders couldn't bend the structures and processes of dealing with corruption, such structures and processes were, for better or worse, eventually bent by global elements.

Conclusion

In Sierra Leone, President Koroma acknowledged that corruption is a culture— a negative one at that—and when he emphasized the fact that corruption is an attitude, he subscribed to the social scientific scholarship that corruption is an act that grows out of an individual will and is through and through egoistical; therefore, it is disrespectful and even anthropologically wrong to think of corruption as the collective will of a people of a given institution, community or nation. Schwenke, in many instances, reminded us that the fight against corruption is itself a political will in that the battle is waged against a concept, a practice that undermines the interest of the common good.

Why the ACC is concerned that we as civil and public servants imbibe ethical values at our workplace? Could the exercise just be an end in itself or a means to an end? Research must have informed the ACC that institutions of government are underperforming in their provisions of service delivery or that no matter how hard MDAs work, their service delivery mechanisms do not maximize in their delivery. The core aim of such a workshop is to bring institutions and their watchdog together to deliberate performance ethics and delivery ethics based on the rule of law so that, as Kauzya noted, "When we say people trust government we may be talking about trust in the sense that the institutions of government are working well and in a predictable way. We may be talking about trust in the sense that people trust the employees of government. We may also be talking about trust in the sense that people trust government because services rendered by the government are well appreciated and equitable (p.11)"

The recent attention that the Sierra Leonean media and civil society organizations showed to the work ethics and work performances of the civil and public servants, where professionally conducted, has served as a third eye on behalf of citizens and taxpayers. As civil and public servants, we sometimes become irritated at the swarming bee attitude of the media and civil society organizations over both our jobs and our lifestyles. If it must make any civil and public servant feel at ease, civil society organizations and the media watch the watcher as much as they watch the watched.

Accountability has almost become a clock hand for every clock hour, if not a dozen clock hands for every clock hour. At times the buzz and the chimes get in the way of the timekeepers. Nevertheless, according to Tadmore and Tetlock (p.9), studies showed that "when individuals are held accountable, they are likely to adopt behaviors that are considered socially acceptable in their particular cultural milieu. Thus people from individualistic culture are likely to display competition whereas people from collectivistic cultures are likely to display cooperation."

The significance of the above quote for our context is that which deals with the cultures of collectivistic societies. For all it is worth, anthropologically speaking, let it be understood that societies of the West are referred to as individualistic cultures while those of Africa are collectivistic. They can also be referred to as high and low context cultures for Africa and the West respectively. This little digression is important only when we insist on a purely African eye view of morality and ethics. You will notice that, for the purpose of our workshop, I have been oscillating between a world view and an African view. The important thing I hope is that, my paper has been able to deliver on the promise of making a case for civil and public servants and their need to uphold ethical values as prevention corruption measure.

References

Couto, R.A. The Science and Philosophy of Political Leadership

Heinze, E. The concept of injustice. Routledge

Kauzya, J. "The human factor in building trust in government: leadership capacity development perspectives in Africa" Presentation at the 2007 International Public Management Association for Human Resources Conference in Cape Town International Convention Center, Cape Town, South Africa 19-20 April 2007.

Lopez-Carlos, A. "The Moral dimensions of corruption" in Future

Development, The World Bankblogs.worldbank.org/futuredevelopment/moral-dimensions-corruption (December 12, 2017).

Schwenke, C. (2003). "Corruption" in Political and civic leadership: A reference handbook (ed.) Richard A. Couto. (in press)

Tadmore & Tetlock. (2003). "Accountability" in Political and civic leadership: A reference handbook (ed.) Richard A. Couto. (in press)

Weber, M http://www.ne.jp/asahi/moriyuki/abukuma/weber/lecture/politics_vocation.html
(December 6, 2017)

White, R.F. Business ethics. http://faculty.msj.edu/whiter/nexusofc ontracts.pdf (December 12, 2017)..

CHAPTER 9

A Taste of Nationhood: A Review of *When the State Fails: Studies on Intervention in the Sierra Leone Civil War* Edited by Tunde Zack Williams (Pluto Press, 2012)

In *When the State Fails: Studies on Intervention in the Sierra Leone Civil War*, the country comes under an intense self-scrutiny. The postmortem seeks to understand the critical agents of democracy in the country's political and economic transition. Across the divide, the majority of Sierra Leoneans are convinced that the ten-year civil war that ate up the country between 1991 and 2001 was as a result of collapsed public institutions first left behind by an exploiting British colonial system and then further destroyed by greedy and visionless African leaders. These institutions, having been destroyed over the years, not only became incapable of enhancing the rule of law, but incapable of ensuring economic production and the garnering of national wealth in any shape or form.

To understand fully the political conflict of any African nation it is helpful to understand the geographical make up of that nation. Topography, borders, landmass, air provisions and aridity affect the shape of a nation's historical and political conflicts. Alongside internal players, Sierra Leone's distant and immediate neighbors played a role both in perpetrating and resolving the ten year political war that consumed the country between 1991 and 2001. For some, like Liberia and Guinea, their roles in the conflict were shaped by the close geographical affinity to Sierra Leone, while others, like the United Kingdom and Nigeria, had affinities that could be better understood in historical globalization terms.

I agree with one of the contributors who cautioned that "States do not become sustainable democracies as a result of external intervention and it is far better to embed institutions in the histories, cultures, needs and interests of the mass publics..." (Kandeh, (92). And true to their arts, the contributors thoroughly researched the local histories, cultures, needs, and interests of the mass publics as the foreground against when they discussed and analyzed the successes and weaknesses of the external intervention in the Sierra Leone civil conflict. Of the many of the recommendations proffered at the end of each chapter, one could see they took the histories, cultures, needs and interests of the Sierra Leoneans into consideration.

Like many of the contributors have pointed out in *When the States Failed*, I will be careful not to toe the line of particularly foreign researchers and writers who have attributed the cause of the Sierra Leone war to struggles over diamonds. While diamonds fueled the war, they were only a means to several ends and not ends in themselves. The foremost advanced reason for the conflict as pointed out by the contributors is the lack of compatible leadership cohesiveness to address the persistent social and economic decadence.

A survey of the political landscape in the aftermath of colonialism throws light on what was primarily responsible for the future civil conflict of 1991 through 2001. Sierra Leone became a modern state after freed slaves were shipped from the Americas and Britain, with the British Crown Colony accompanying to establish the first national government under the authority of the British monarchy (Davies 2002). Throughout the reign of the British, the thorny issue of uniting the former slaves with their indigenous countrymen and women remained unachievable. So that by the time the country demanded political independence, the seeds of disunity had germinated, especially following the unwillingness of the British to grant Sierra Leoneans their independence, and the former's undiplomatic and corrupt method of transferring political power in disregard of the ethnic tension they had helped to brew (Hallowell 2006).

Soon after the British left, political rivalries broke out, first between descendants of the former slaves, known as the krio and the indigenes, the country's two largest ethnic groups, the Themne and the Mende. A researcher outside of this volume (2004), summarized the divide as "The Sierra Leone People's Party (SLPP) ruling since independence came to be perceived as biased towards the south-eastern regions, home to the Mendes accounting for 30% of the population, and other smaller ethnic groups. The Northern regions, home to the Temnes, also accounting for 30% of the population, and other smaller ethnic groups, rallied round the All People's Congress (APC)" (p.4).

As the contributors noted in various ways, when class and ethnic struggles became the central definition of politics in Sierra Leone in the 1980s, there were discontents all over the place. Traditionalist republicans referred to the movement as a coup d'état by a few highly placed individuals to defraud and hijack the state. Every post-colonial country in Sub-Saharan Africa, including Sierra Leone relegated both political and economic agencies to the state as the best custodian of the people's collective property against any likely external aggression or internal civil war.

Sheldon S. Wolin, another researcher outside of this volume, helps us to understand the elusive nature of boundaries and classifications in democratic societies. These classifications are strong metaphors examining class division in developing democracies and liberalist outlook. Perhaps Wolin's most famous statement is "…democracy is too simple for complex societies and too complex for simple ones" (Wolin, p. 42) In this case, the Sierra Leone democracy obviously falls under the category of simple societies. -Certainly, good democracies are a network of connectivity, requiring the existence and sustenance of multiple agencies. Where these agencies are unequal in the society, governmental policies are usually improperly formed and executed.

It could be misleading though to think that Sierra Leone is a simple society. Assuming a neoliberal position, each of the contributors in this volume engaged in the web-design of dissecting the complexities of a country into which all forms of interventions poured to save it from being a failed state. The question is was Sierra Leone ever a failed state? At what point in history did it fail? Whether one agrees with the contributors or not that Sierra Leone failed at some point, the important thing about this book is that it is at once the dictionary of our civil conflict as given to us by Sierra Leoneans!

References

Wolin, S. (1996). Fugitive democracy. In S. Benhabib (Ed.). *Democracy and difference: Contesting the Boundaries of the Political* (31-45). Princeton University Press.

CHAPTER 10

Toward a Creative Liberal Education
The College Lecturer in Post-Conflict Sierra Leone a lecture delivered at the Fatima Institute, Makeni, Sierra Leone,
October 27, 2007

I have spent the last several years teaching university and college education, first in the United States and now in Sierra Leone. In the United States, I taught at two community colleges and a university. Since returning to Sierra Leone, I have briefly taught at Fourah Bay College (FBC), before joining the faculty at the Institute of Public Administration and Management (IPAM), constituent colleges of the University of Sierra Leone. Variously, I have taught in the liberal arts/social sciences departments, instructing in modules ranging from general writing skills to research writing, from modules bordering on critical thinking, to those in the social sciences at both undergraduate and graduate levels. You will notice that I have refused to call these modules by their traditional names, such as, English, Sociology and Philosophy. The backgrounds from which I come behave in the same way. In both my masters and in my on-going doctoral program, I got exposed to what is known as an interdisciplinary education. My university education shifted a little from what the quintessential traditional university offers.

Built on the modular system, semester after semester, students oscillate from one academic discipline to another, until they are made aware of the interdisciplinarity existing among academic disciplines at the tertiary level. Many universities in the United States that offer this kind of education have argued that students are better prepared to face the challenges of the practical world. At the same time, hundreds and hundreds of traditional universities and colleges are incorporating a good portion of the interdisciplinarity system. With an introduction such as mine for a discourse at this level, one can expect many theses to emerge. Today's lecture has as its thesis that the growth and relevance of tertiary education in post-conflict Sierra Leone largely depends on lecturers' determination to develop personally as well as professionally, by tapping into local resources, and by allowing the outcomes of their research to inform their instructions.

After all, what does lecture mean? The term lecture, a 14th century coinage, comes from the Latin expression *lectus*, the past participle of *legere*, to write. Some people have referred to it as the action of reading, and others, a discourse on a given issue before an audience. By the 1950s, the term *lectern*, a reading desk, was considered a cousin-relation to the term lecture. We notice here that these dictions form an association of words that builds in one's mind the picture of an inquirer engaged in the art of inquiry. At once the college lecturer is a creativity trainer. It is difficult for learning to occur where an imagination has not been fired! Perhaps one difference between the school teacher and the college lecturer is that the former builds the door for the learner to open it whiles the latter opens the door for the learner to enter into it. I have used the metaphor of the door for two reasons: firstly, and ironically also, to indicate that knowledge though scattered all around us, is a hidden treasure that can only be found when one agrees to step into the threshold and not step away from it; secondly, that because knowledge is a treasure hidden behind a door, both lecturers and their students, perpetually engaged in the art of opening doors and entering into them, are together, learners. Education at the tertiary level must be approached as if an invention is underway. But of course tertiary education is all about invention. Booth et al in their work *The Craft of Research* (2003) tell us that "Even experienced researchers feel anxious when they tackle a new project, especially when it's of a new kind."

Let us now attempt to form a picture of the structure of university lectureship in Sierra Leone. I almost decided against making this task part of my lecture for the simple reason that until I left Sierra Leone for the United States some seven years ago, I knew nothing about lecturers beyond what the simple eyes of a student is exposed to. We are not making an assessment of university policies governing lecturers and lectureship. Rather, we are having a cursory view of the lecturer in our socio-cultural and economic context. Against Sierra Leone's poor economic backdrop, the university lecturer is faced with a thousand and one challenges within and without the classroom. Figuratively speaking, university lecturers find themselves limited to a forty hour work a week schedule, meaning that, the job of a lecturer for all it is worth cumulates its results based on contact hours with students. When students tell you that they enjoyed a certain lecture, they are telling you that the lecturer has a deep understanding of the discipline as it is traditionally laid out and has successfully passed over the material to them considerably well.

But what is wrong with that idea? Isn't lecture supposed to be just that? What else should lecturers do other than instructing students in ideas they themselves have been instructed in? Wouldn't it therefore be true to say that the best university students would be those capable, without the value of lecture notes that had been granted, to remember all that the lecturer had passed on to them the entire semester, and in a three hour hall of examination spill all the contents? We shall return to these concerns later.

Bridging the gap between the students and the college corporation, the lecturer is the ignition key of the motor. If the question "What happens now?" is posed on any college campus, it is directed at the lecturer. The administration would say that they have provided the wherewithal for a sound lecture to occur, and now it is up to the lecturer to deliver a sound lecture; the students would say they have honored all that was to honor, and now it is up to the lecturer to deliver a sound lecture. I used to think that everyone gathers on college campuses because of the student body. No, everyone, including the student body, gathers there because of the lecturer. If lecturers, like Socrates or the Sophists of ancient Greece, choose to lecture off campus, it is but wise for the knowledge-hungry student to accompany them.

Of the three units I have mentioned above, the administration, the lecturer and the student body, the lecturer has the most tasking assignment. The administration is always there to provide the wherewithal to make things happen, the student body always only has to arrive. The lecturer arrives on campus or should arrive on campus with something 'new.' When lecturers think that, well, after all we are now educated; all we need to do now is to 'teach,' they take away from themselves the miracle of the long-thirst, which I have also called, un-pejoratively speaking, *the theory of the congosa, (congosa, a Krio term, here being a metaphor for perpetual intellectual hunger)*; that value of being the driver they are supposed to be. Wouldn't it be ridiculous for bus drivers, with the lives of many people on board their buses to say that, well the bus is already made; all we have to do now is only to drive? Shouldn't they check for possible break failure or fuel running low? Similarly, university lecturers always have to be as dynamic as the community in which they live in.

I have subtitled this lecture as "the college lecturer in post-conflict Sierra Leone." What does a lecturer who merely occupies a small room and talks to less than a hundred students at any one time have to do with the grand matters of post-conflict Sierra Leone? And for that matter, how do lectures at Fatima Institute, a rural university, affect political will in post-conflict Sierra Leone? Coming from an exhausting decade long war, Sierra Leone needs to rebuild its self-confidence. You have heard it said in many quarters in this country that the youth are in the majority and that they should be allowed to be players in the country's political process as early in their lives as possible. Politicians have only paid lip service to this appeal, but the classrooms have provided a forum for the youth. While the brutal aspect of the war might have ended, too many questions regarding scholarship and academia remain at warring postures. It may seem that scientific discovery is responsible for America's dominance of the world; however, America's continued superiority is as a result of that country's liberal thinking and practices of the social sciences both in America and in the world at large. What makes the whole thing interesting is that American national politics is as much in university classrooms as it is in the White House and in the Capitol. Rodolfo Stravenhagen in an essay, "Decolonizing the Social Sciences" argued that:

It lies perhaps in the destiny of the social sciences that they should not only reflect the dominant forms of social organization of their times, but also—as they have done ever since they grew out of the social and political thought of the Enlightenment—that they should become major vehicles for the expression of the radical countercurrents and critical conscience that these very forms of organization have brought forth. This dialectical relationship between the social sciences and society finds its way into the ambiguous and frequently conflictive roles that social scientists as individuals are called upon to play in modern society."

I might want to add that in post-conflict Sierra Leone university lecturers in the social sciences and in the humanities should seek to decolonize university humanities and social sciences and modify them in other that they can be relevant to the Sierra Leone situation. At present, it could be argued that NGO's and civil society organizations are, anthropologically speaking, more in tune with the dynamic forces engaged in the social structures and fabric in Sierra Leone than are university lecturers. These organizations are playing the role of the university lecturer. The Sierra Leone university system continues not only to be elitist in structure, but to be *largely* and *exclusively* dependent on Western books, experiences and theories to find explanations for socio-cultural activities in Sierra Leone. Stravenhagen has quoted Karl Marx as saying that "Theory becomes a material force as soon as it has gripped the masses." What does this mean in concrete terms? Imagine a Western theory that has been taught at a Sierra Leone university for the longest time, yet has no practical reference in the lives of the people, at least not in any apparent terms. Would such a theory become a material force? Stravenhagen further nails the problem:

> …in most cases, scholars in academia communities (particularly when they go back to their own foreign countries) can do relatively little to control the uses or misuses (or simply the non-use) of the fruits of their labour. We often hear it said amongst radicals that social scientific produce is really only of use to repressive governments, the exploiting classes or the self-seeking imperialists."

How does the lecturer fit into this accusation? We had earlier established that even though the university primarily exists for the sake of the students, yet the learning activities are engineered by the lecturers. Lecturers are to be rather considered sources of fountain and not themselves fountains. All throughout this time our aim is to discuss the readiness agenda of the Sierra Leone post-conflict college lecturer. Before this time, it was possible for lecturers to be a 'passive' force in the learning process. This tendency occurs when lecturers merely perceive their position as being only a means to an end. In today's Sierra Leone, lecturers have to figure themselves in a more engaging term. Stravenhagen has noted that most scholars and intellectuals, particularly those returning from the Western world to their developing countries have not been able to monitor their scholarship in other to minimize what kind of knowledge can result to a miss-education of their countrymen and women. Leszek Kolakowski, writing about a radical kind of research theory called positivism in an essay

"An Overview of Positivism" states that Positivism

> ...stands for a certain philosophical attitude to human knowledge; strictly speaking, it does not prejudge questions about how men arrive at knowledge. But it is a collection of rules and evaluative criteria referring to human knowledge: it tells us what kind of contents in our statements about the world deserve the name of knowledge and supplies us with norms that make it possible to distinguish between that which may and that which may not reasonably be asked.

Isn't this thinking elemental of Enlightenment periods? Our present period is perhaps the most exciting period in Sierra Leone second only to the period of independence. I returned to Sierra Leone in 2007 and was greeted by many emerging post-conflict educational institutions. For a long while, everyone went to Fourah Bay College, Njala University or the Milton Margai College. Two of those colleges took the rural student to Freetown and unto all that city's attendant hassles. Of the post-conflict emergent educational institutions, many are technical colleges that cater for the vocational tradesperson. Perhaps the Fatima Institute is the only post-conflict tertiary institution that is in scholarship and academia; a college placed on the rural breasts of a rural culture. The stakeholders of this fine institution, and these include lecturers and students, therefore have the task ahead of them to not only redefine theoretic education, but to negotiate a fine nexus between theory and practice in their local communities. Ali Mazrui, one of Africa's finest minds writes about the seven functions of culture, and I might add, of lecturers of culture in his book *Cultural forces in World Politics*

> "Culture," he writes, "serves seven fundamental functions in society. First, it helps to provide lenses of *perception* and *cognition*. How people view the world is greatly conditioned by one or more cultural paradigms to which they have been exposed...

> "The second function of culture lies in providing *motives for human behavior*. What makes a person respond behaviorally in a particular manner is partly cultural in origin…
>
> "The third function of culture lies in providing criteria of *evaluation*. What is deemed better or worse, ugly or beautiful, moral or immoral, attractive or repulsive, is partly a child of culture...
>
> The fourth function of culture is to provide a *basis of identity*. Ethnic nepotism is itself a product of culture in this identity…
>
> Fifthly, culture is a *mode of communication*. Culture as a communication can take forms—including music, the performing arts, and the wider world of ideas…
>
> The sixth function of culture is as a *basis of stratification*. Class, rank and status are profoundly conditioned by cultural variables. University education became a major factor in redefining status and gradation in modern African societies…
>
> The seventh function of culture lies in the system of production and consumption. Patterns of consumption sometimes affect production as profoundly as production helps to shape consumption…

Western education came to Africa like a Trojan horse. We were amazed at the imported knowledge from the West to an extent that we thought of knowledge as being truth in a Kantian sense. We saw ourselves as consumers of final products, products that were manufactured in the West and brought to us in giant cargo ships. The West came to us in the guise of pre-Socratic Greek philosophers like Parmenide whose "poem depicted the philosopher as an initiate who has received insight into the truth from a goddess who holds the keys of justice in her hands;" also, like Empedocles who "claimed special knowledge on the basis of his own long cycle of incarnations as 'a boy, a girl, a bush, a bird, and a dumb sea fish;'" also, like Heraclitus who "compared his pithy aphorisms to the sayings of the Delphic oracle, implying that they contained a hidden wisdom that the listener must work to extract;" also, like Pythagoras whose followers thought of him "as a wonder-working sage, and formed communities bound by vows of silence to perpetuate his wisdom."

Let me say a little about the University of Sierra Leone—in particular, Fourah Bay College. Although the University of Sierra Leone has existed for over a century yet it has always been an alien institution to the majority of Sierra Leoneans. No less a person than the former Vice chancellor, Professor Kosonike Koso-Thomas admitted at a university congregation in 1998 as follows:

> Mr. Chancellor, being at this congregation without the many of our countrymen who hardly know of our university and what it does, and who even have no means of listening to the broadcast of these proceedings, I should feel inconsequential. I know that this ceremony touches not even the fringe of their existence and represent nothing compatible with the quality and style."

> In the true sense of the word, a university is supposed be, as Professor Koso-Thomas rightly said: "a defiant breed, who are accustomed to pursuing our investigations in any direction in which our intellect leads, and make public our findings, irrespective of political and other interests."

The question therefore is where do we place the university system in the Sierra Leone community? There doesn't seem to be any physical or psychological relationship between the university system and the larger Sierra Leonean community. It is as if both are meant to function independent of the other. But in reality the university system is more aware of the community than the community is aware of the university system. Never does it so easily dawn on grassroots Sierra Leoneans that the university system exists to help them grow into informed and better people if they don't have to go through its educational program. On the other hand, rather than the university system seeing itself, vis-à-vis the community, as a partner in development, it has always assumed a superior status. It considers itself the light of the nation. There is nothing wrong in the university system thinking itself the light of society; but to assume that status, the feeling should be mutually expressed by the society in which the university is placed. It is therefore not surprising that the larger community, disgusted with the supremacist and elitist education and thinking of our national universities, have condemned the university with cynical remarks like *nar sense make buk, nor to book make sense*. Aiah Gbakima, currently Vice Chancellor and Principle of the University of Sierra Leone was long aware of the problem with university scholarship. In an essay titled "How Can the Educational Services in Sierra Leone Be Rescued?" he lamented that

The University should be a place of learning; a place to nurture students and challenge their creativity. Majority of the administrative and academic staff were not only complacent and unproductive, they lacked the zeal and the energy to improve themselves professionally. Most seldom thought about writing grant proposals to enhance their careers because they were already tenured after a few years of service. They expected the government to provide everything necessary for their work. Most refuse to criticize constructively, even when they knew something was wrong and not in the interest of the University, because of the fear that they may be denied tenure or promotion. The do-nothing and keep your job approach gradually ate away the University's ability and in effect, the country's ability to invest in her own people. A clear manifestation of laziness was what the students referred to as a *legacy*, where the lecturer uses the same lecture notes year after year. In essence, there is no improvement in the material presented and one student passes the notes to the next generation of incoming students."

What Gbakima refers to as a *legacy* my generation of students at the then Milton Margai Teachers College, and I understand it still is so today, called *ngeigba*, a Mende terminology meaning—a recycling of old lecture notes. The origin of such traditional lecture notes at the Milton Margai College could be traced to lecture notes in various departments at Fourah Bay College and Njala University College, then both constituent colleges of the University of Sierra Leone. The majority of lecturers at Milton Margai College were drawn from the University of Sierra Leone, the only institution then that offered academic degrees. Most people even traced some of these legacies to specific lecturers. Lecture notes in literature have been traced to Professors Eldred Durosimi Jones and Eustace Palmer, mathematics lecture notes to Professor Labour, etc, etc. In fact, the most compelling argument the college administration and students of Milton Margia College made for their college to be upgraded to a university was that education at Milton Margai College was by way of contents similar in level to those at Njala University College and Fourah Bay College. Students, who later enrolled in the two latter institutions for the benefit of university degrees, not only took along with them their Milton Margai lecture notes, but exempted themselves from further note taking, yet made prominent presences among the best graders in those institutions. Gbakima further talks about a negative kind of culture that seemed to have emerged in academia with regards to laziness and critical analysis. There can be no doubt that education in the humanities and social sciences have thriven on critical analysis. Any student deprived of this value can be said to have been miss-educated. In fact, when lecturers notice that their students have become heavily dependent on lecture notes, they should at once revisit and restructure their teaching methodologies, and fashion them in a more democratic pattern as to allow the students to be in the center of the learning process. Lecturers should inspire students to challenge the texts, challenge the instructions, and challenge their peers.

College lecturers should be pro-active in the classroom as well as in the community. Take the theories to the community—the community to the classroom and crossbreed the two. Germinate new thinking in African anthropology and other social sciences. Engage in what is known as the Socratic Inquiry. University lecturers should conduct research and publish their findings. A few of my colleagues have told me that they always wanted to write but that there were no publishing outlets. I tell them that waiting for big corporate publishers to accept their material would be futile; I let them realize that the lecturer's best potential of being "published" is in the classroom. Conduct local research and share your writing with your peers and with your students. Many great writers of old did not see their work in print. Most valuable writings were stored in university libraries and archives for years before others identified them as gems and published them in later life. Getting published is not really the issue, but getting read by students. A modern America philosopher, John Rawls, in his book, *A Theory of Justice* appropriates the college lecturer in the following terms

Each generation must not only preserve the gains of culture and civilization, and maintain intact those just institutions that have been established, but it must also put aside in each period of time a suitable amount of real capital accumulation. This saving may take various forms from net investment in machinery and other means of production to investment in learning and education.

Of course not many people have a democratic idea of such dynamic scholarship and academia in our communities outside the university system. Noted among this set are politicians and state rulers. Nussbaum cautions that "When intellectuals behave this (liberal) way, the people they intend to benefit are not always happy. To people who are deeply immersed in practical affairs, especially in a democracy, the questioning intellectual—especially, perhaps, the philosopher—is always a slightly suspect character." We know about the Greek Tribunal putting Socrates to death for, as they put it, corrupting the minds of the young. A similar fate has befallen intellectuals, generation after generation. But we as lecturers in Sierra Leone today can assume that we have left the worst of our civil conflict behind us—in fact, we can always suggest that we are now academic peace ambassadors, researching our every cultural movements to understand what took us to war, and what we as a people can do to avert war amongst us forever.

References

Booth, W.C. et al (2003). *The Craft of Research*, (2nd ed.) The University of Chicago Press: Chicago, p.3

Stravenhagen, R. (1993). "Decolonizing Applied Social Sciences" in *Social Research: Philosophy, Politics and Practice*, (ed) Martyn Hammersley, SAGE Publications: London, p.52

Kolakowski, L. (1993). "An Overall View of Positivism" in *Social Research: Philosophy, Politics and Practice*, (ed) Martyn Hammersley, SAGE Publications: London, p.2

Mazrui, A. (1990). *Cultural Forces in World Politics*, James Currey: Oxford, p.7-8

Nussbaum, M. (1997). *Cultivating Humanity: A Classical Defense of Reform in Liberal Education*, Harvard University Press: Cambridge, p.20

Koso-Thomas, K. (1988). University of Sierra Leone Congregation

Gbakima, A. (2000). "How Can the Educational Services be Rescued?" in *International Journal of Sierra Leone Studies & Reviews*, Maiden Issue, Vol. 1 No. 1 Fall, Department of Communications School of Arts & Sciences, Bowie State University: Maryland, p.92

Rawls, J. (1971). *A Theory of Justice*, Harvard University Press: Cambridge, p.285

Nussbaum, M. (1997). *Cultivating Humanity: A Classical Defense of Reform in Liberal Education*, Harvard University Press: Cambridge, p.21

Media Foundation for West Africa (MFWA)'s network of lawyers meets in Accra. March 31, 2009. www.mediafound.org/index.php?option=com_content&task=view&id=325 (retrieved September 2, 2009).

Press Statement: ECOWAS Court dismisses Gambian government objection. June 30, 2009. www.mediafound.org/index.php?option=com_content&task=view&id=388 (retrieved September 2, 2009).

Daniel, Isioma, "I Lit the Match" in The Guardian. Monday, February 17, 2003. guardian.co.uk/world/2003/feb/17/gender.pressandpublishing (retrieved September 2, 2009).

Rawls, John. (1971). *A Theory of Justice*. Harvard University Press: Cambridge

Howard, Ross. Conflict Sensitive Journalism: A Handbook: International Media Support

Mill, J.S. (1861). "Utilitarianism" in *Philosophical Classics; From Plato to Nietzsche*. (ed) Forrest Baird and Walter Kaufmann. (1997). Prentice Hall: New Jersey. P.998.

Rawls, John. (1971). *A Theory of Justice*. Harvard University Press: Massachusetts. P.127.
Kant, I. (1785). "Foundation for the Metaphysics of Morals" in *Philosophical Classics; From Plato to Nietzsche*. (ed) Forrest Baird and Walter Kaufmann. (1997). Prentice Hall: New Jersey. P.900.
Kant, I. (1785). "Foundation for the Metaphysics of Morals" in *Philosophical Classics; From Plato to Nietzsche*. (ed) Forrest Baird and Walter Kaufmann. (1997). Prentice Hall: New Jersey. P.901.
Mill, J.S. (1861). "Utilitarianism" in *Philosophical Classics; From Plato to Nietzsche*. (ed) Forrest Baird and Walter Kaufmann. (1997). Prentice Hall: New Jersey. P.992.
Rawls, John. (1971). *A Theory of Justice*. Harvard University Press: Massachusetts. P.141.
Johnson, I. Lecture on Aristotle's Nicomachaen ethics, delivered, in part, in Liberal Studies 301, on November 18, 1997. P.3.
Kant, I. (1785). "Foundation for the Metaphysics of Morals" in *Philosophical Classics; From Plato to Nietzsche*. (ed) Forrest Baird and Walter Kaufmann. (1997). Prentice Hall: New Jersey. P.998.
Noddings, N. (1995). "Ethics and Caring" in *Justice and Care: Essential Readings in feminist Ethics*. Westview Press: Colorado. P.9..

CHAPTER 11

Theorizing African Narrative Mediation of Conflict Resolution through Poems, Songs and Stories

This essay argues that the narrative mediation model, which is considered a post-modernist and constructionist model in the West, is actually an African Narrative Indigenous Model (ANIM). The essay further gives a description of the model, suggesting that its characteristic nature as practiced in Africa can only enrich the Western format of narrative mediation model.

In the catholic framework of mediation, the following three approaches have been identified: (1) the problem solving mediation model, (2) the transformative mediation model, and (3) the narrative mediation model. Depending on the nature of the conflict that is being mediated, mediators usually entertain bias for or against one model or the other. Among factors that affect any mediator's preference are culture, environment, and education on one hand and the various other kinds of challenges posed by the conflict itself on the other.

The narrative mediation model deals with conflict through the stories that participants narrate. Then, the mediators and disputants, through the processed messages and meta-messages, recreate every story to come up with the alternative story. This model is a relatively new concept in the West. Theorists are still digging deeply into the model's characteristic nature. It is very easy to notice, therefore, that answers are still required as to the relationship between conflict and storytelling on the one hand, and storytelling and conflict narrative on the other hand. It is becoming clearer to researchers that the narrative mediation model can only be better understood when studied in a cultural context. Do experiences in Africa matter in understanding this seemingly new dispensation?

Keywords: Narrative mediation, mediators, conflict, storytelling, poems, songs, culture

---

In the catholic framework of mediation, the following three approaches have been identified: (1) the problem solving mediation model, (2) the transformative mediation model, and (3) the narrative mediation model. Depending on the nature of the conflict that is being mediated, mediators usually entertain bias for or against one model or the other. Among factors that affect any mediator's preference are culture, environment, and education on one hand and the various other kinds of challenges posed by the conflict itself on the other.

Let us briefly examine the three models of mediation. The problem solving model is said to be the earliest of the three models. Winslade and Monk (2000) question the frame of mind under which this model has been subjected. They argue that people who lean toward this model interpret conflict in light of the frustration of "human need and interest" (p.32). The problem solving model is no doubt a derivative from the litigation process that focuses on addressing the human desire rather than the human factor. According to Moore (2003), the transformative model puts a premium on the human factor in order to improve on the human bonding at all levels of disputes. Mediators and disputants work toward discovering or rediscovering a new level of understanding of the macro-relationship through the conflict. The narrative mediation model deals with conflict through the stories that participants narrate. Then, the mediators and disputants, through the processed messages and meta-messages, recreate every story to come up with the alternative story. This model is a relatively new concept in the West. Theorists are still digging deeply into the model's characteristic nature. It is very easy to notice, therefore, that answers are still required as to the relationship between conflict and storytelling on the one hand, and storytelling and conflict narrative on the other hand. It is becoming clearer to researchers that the narrative mediation model can only be better understood when studied in a cultural context. Do experiences in Africa matter in understanding this seemingly new dispensation?

In 2001, John Winslade and Gerald Monk published a beautiful book on mediation titled *Narrative Mediation: A New Approach to Conflict Resolution*. Perhaps if these authors had known about conflict resolution in Africa, they would have safely subtitled their book "A New Approach to Conflict Resolution *in the West.*"

The book, metaphorically speaking, forces an old model into a new wine skin. The narrative mediation model is, perhaps, the oldest and most encompassing of the three most prominent models in the West. Maybe, I should mention here that, as far as Africa is concerned, what the West has divided into the problem solving mediation model and the transformative mediation model are rather an extension of the narrative mediation model. However, anyone can understand why new models are ever on the increase in this field of study. As human behaviors and societies grow more and more complex, it has become necessary to provide for the many different categories of people who, without choice, must live side by side with each other in this equally ever crowded global village.

A good mediator should particularly be wary about the challenges posed by conflicts. A mediator should not lose sight of the physical as well as the psychological picture of a conflict when determining what mediation model to use that can best achieve positive outcomes. It must be noted that positive outcomes do not necessarily mean win/win situations. When mediating, the mediator looks out for pointers, parameters, and goals to be achieved before he or she can consider a mediation process as being successful.

Mediation is not necessarily entered into in order to avoid litigation costs. Sometimes even disputants can agree to enter into mediation for cases under litigation. While litigation looks out for angles in a conflict that could lead one party over another in order to achieve a win/lose situation, both litigants and the court system can at times be astounded as to why such conflicts never really come to a conclusion. At the same time, mediators sometimes puzzle over why some conflicts don't budge, even with the application of different mediation models.

Recently, the West 'discovered' a third mediation model, the narrative. Winslade and Monk have celebrated the narrative mediation model as being the best and most post-modern. By way of thesis, this paper will show not only that the narrative mediation model is traditionally an indigenous model, but also it will show that the model had its origin in Africa.

The Nature and Scope of African Conflicts

African conflicts can be conveniently divided into conflicts of the village square, and they include political, border, ideological, and spiritual disputes; and conflicts of the farm. They also include marriage, kinship, and rivalry. Although Africa is not unique under this categorization, I want to point out that conflicts are structured by the cultural settings in which they occur. Augsburger (1992) reminds us, "in the study of conflict we move into the mysterious sides of culture, the depths that are revealed in threat, emergency, competition, and confrontation" (p.16). That movement results to a backward-forward understanding of both the conflict and relationship and of any implication to their termination or continuation. The narrative mediation model uses the storytelling technique in mediation. Unlike the problem solving and the transformative models, both of which put a premium on certain aspects of the processes, the narrative approach endorses the Aristotelian model of speaker, argument, and audience with equal importance. In the narrative approach, the characters are as important as the plot, setting, the images, and symbols used in the process. When these literary elements neatly come into play, what Winslade and Monk (2003) calls the three phases, "engagement, deconstructing the conflict-saturated story, and constructing the alternative story" (p.58) are achieved. The question might rise as to why we need that much loaded a package in mediation. Maiese (2005) who reminds us that our worldviews are shaped by our view of our communities, cautions us that "These frames are typically unconscious and non-reflective and help to shape the way in which individuals make sense of their world's meaning in somewhat different ways, it is not surprising that their ways of coming to know and understand conflict likewise are different" (p.2).

Mediation in an African Context

Although it is increasingly becoming fashionable for scholars to argue that high context and low context cultures are no longer based on geographical determinants, this paper will insist that contextually and culturally speaking, much of Africa is still decidedly high context. In this regard, I shall add to Mazrui's claim (1999) that "Territorially, the United States expanded as a state but not as an empire and Britain expanded as an empire but not as a state and that Africa neither expanded as a homogenous state of Western construct nor reduced of its indigenous heterogeneity. Recently, with the beginning of the famous Truth and Reconciliation Commission (TRC) in South Africa after apartheid, other African post-conflict countries like Sierra Leone are helping to institutionalize the TRC in the continent. However, only a few miles into the process, many complaints have been made about the effectiveness of the program. For instance, the Sierra Leone TRC is far from being successful. Video tapes show victims and perpetrators placed in wrong contexts and settings poorly managed, and with the application of the problem solving model, couched in strange linguistic paradigm. The entire process ends up inflicting a more abusive scar on the victims of the conflict. As with the South African experience, every TRC organized on the continent has failed and will continue to fail as long as organizers continue to ignore the African indigenous method of narrative mediation model.

Narrative Mediation as an African Model

In recent scholarship, the origin of the narrative mediation model has been traced to Australia. Hansen (2003) informs us that narrative mediation came out of a Narrative Family Therapy, a 1980s program developed by Michael White and David Epston in Australia. Hansen further tells us that these two Australians discovered narrative mediation through their interest in post-modernism and constructionism and examining the making of meaning through the filter of language and subjective interpretation of facts (p.1). Did mediation take its impetus in Western cultures, or could the mostly high context aboriginal cultures of Australia have informed White and Epston's discovery of narrative mediation? Could Hansen and others have merely been shortsighted in approximating the origin of narrative mediation? In the case of non-Western conflicts, LeBaron succinctly states

High context cultures feature collective identity-focus covert communication and homogeneity. In high context cultures communication tends to be assertive. This means that more attention is paid to the context of communication, including behaviour and environment, the relationship between the messenger and receiver, the messenger's family history and status, and so on. This approach is said to prevail in Asian countries including Japan, China and Korea, as well as Latin America and Africa (p7).

Take our cues from LeBaron, we shall examine the nature of communication in the narrative mediation model. Both the problem solving and the transformative mediation models require the parties and the mediators to consider language as the metaphor of negotiation. They both rely on connectivity through communication messages in order to understand the nature of the conflict on the table. In both models, language is the vehicle of assumption; parties depend on language and psychology to recreate the conflict in order to understand it. The danger is that sometimes what carries over is not the conflict. Consequently, set in a high context culture and used in a conflict that involves farmlands, for instance, negative transformation could result and cause disastrous outcomes. For people in high context cultures, the two models have no depth: thus, they are relationally unfulfilling. It must be noted that conflict mediation itself is a social dynamism. In a truly African context, the mediation process is not a private enterprise. Therefore, by the process and each time it is carried out, it touches the lives of many people.

Although the narrative mediation model requires storytelling, the two are not the same. Whereas the storytelling is the process of unfolding, the narrative act is the political metaphor of negotiation. Therefore, as LeBaron states, behavior and environment are elementally useful tools to the process. Perhaps, to understand the narrative mediation model, we must first submit answers to the following questions: What is storytelling? How assertive is it as a tool of mediation?

Africa is perhaps the most culturally diversified continent in the world. "It has been calculated that there exists between 700 and 1250 distinct languages within sub-Saharan West Africa, an area itself larger than Western Europe" (Frazer, 1986, p.7). Such Babel of a land requires a common physical body language to ease the linguistic problems of cross communication that these ethnically based spoken languages pose. In mediating conflicts, therefore, cognizance must be taken of body language expressions and community symbols and images.

Is Narrative Mediation a Post-Modernist or Constructionist Model?

Perhaps a first entry into the narrative mediation model is to enquire into its history and emergence. Added to the model's Australian attachment, Western scholars and practitioners have labeled it as a post-modernist and constructionist approach. An understanding of the characteristic nature of a low context culture can explain why the narrative mediation model could not be Western orientation. A low context culture is individualistic and focuses more on the written language. LeBaron wrote, "Mediation in dominant cultures of North America tends to be characterized by overt communication, structured confrontation" (p.8). This difference between low context and the high context cultures explains why the Sierra Leone Truth and Reconciliation Commission (TRC) organized after that country's decade long civil war did not achieve its intended immediate mandate. The victims were encouraged to be confrontational by ways of overt communication through the problem-solving mediation model that the mediators applied. Confrontationalism in conflict resolution is not integrally African. "Outsiders" fail to realize that "so-called primitive societies often have conflict solutions that are more effective in bonding adversaries and blending goals than those groups who designate themselves as advanced, developed, or possessing far more data about human relations" (Augsburger, 1992, p.6).

One can, therefore, understand why the West, when it recently discovered the narrative mediation model, lauded it as post-modernist and constructionist. Inappropriate classifications such as the one ascribed to the narrative mediation model has led the philosopher, Wright (2000), to write, "During the early twentieth century, the conventional wisdom changed. The ranking of some societies as "higher" than others seemed increasingly unsavory, especially to scholars on the left" (p.14).

What is Storytelling, and what is Its Significance?

As I stated above, storytelling is the process of unfolding through a series of connected and orchestrated events. In storytelling, the past becomes a fountain from which conflict parties tap. Storytelling is a banking process in which the parties have invested, and since the art of mediation is itself a healing process, parties help each other to see all sides of the conflict. There is a connection between war and peace. They both engage people. Karen (2001) talks about anger as being "a means of staying connected instead of lapsing into depression and resentment or both" (p.83). African communities are bonded by the metaphorical emotions of fire and water. The human wire must always have its connecting, cross-transmitting current. Katz and Lawyer (1992) call this situation "submission" by which conflicting parties agree to willingly open up their privacies to the larger community.

Therefore, in appropriating the present and the future, the past becomes a sacred memory of happenings about which mediators should like to hear. Conflict itself is a plot of events that usually constitutes a number of encounters. A conflict must have the characteristic of a story before it can be considered a conflict. There should be a beginning, middle, and an end. They are the complex threads that must neatly entwine. The process of narrative mediation can achieve a double success in which the conflicting parties, through the process of storytelling, can heal their own wounds by adding to the healing processes that the mediators apply to the conflict. The following is a very powerful description of community response to community concerns, (Achebe, 1994).

> The whole village turned out on the *ilo*, men, women and children. They stood round in a huge circle leaving the center of the playground free. The elders and grandees of the village sat on their own stools brought by their young sons or slaves. Okwonkwo was among them. All others stood

> except those who came early enough to secure places on the few strands which had been built by placing smooth logs on forked pillars (p.46).

Even in our popular age of Western domination, there are thousands of African communities that still use the art of traditional storytelling to resolve their conflicts. Because storytelling is a very powerful presence in African communities, we shall now consider some of the many reasons for the sustenance of this art form:

Storytelling as a community unifier: Storytelling is a strong unifier of African peoples. Communities, clans, and families agree to come together to settle their conflicts through the art of storytelling. The success of mediation is not necessarily counted in the number of conflict parties embracing each other, but in parties given the opportunity to dig into their pasts, and discover the many lines of lineages that connect them as families. For instance, conflicts between villages are sometimes easily negotiated when parties discover that the family which founded one of the villages was also the founder of the other village. This discovery automatically makes the conflicting parties see themselves as blood relatives.

Storytelling as a forger of future relationships: The African mediation process is not a private affair. Because many non-conflicting or indirect parties are allowed to sit in, the stories parties narrate could wind around everyone present, occasionally and unintentionally bringing out into the open related conflicts that can be resolved there and then as well (most conflicts in Africa, interpersonal or community conflict, are chain conflicts). Also, the storytelling art helps communities, clans, and families to forge new relationships, thus leading to stronger communities.

Storytelling as a medium to appease the gods and the dead: Through the art of storytelling, communities are able to sing praises to their gods and to remember their brave clansmen and women who may have died as a result of conflict. As a way of making peace, the conflicting parties can agree to recognize the casualties as legendary figures.

Storytelling as a means of preserving history: For a very long time, when the art of writing was not so popular in sub-Sahara Africa, oral transmission was the means of passing the history and literature on to the next generation. To involve many people in community and personal affairs was fashionable then because these very people, especially the young, were the ones who lived longer and understood their societies. When they too were old, they passed their knowledge, including that of conflict resolution, on to their younger generation.

Storytelling as a means of moral instruction: For a long time, many communities in Africa did not have formal education, except the occasional secret societies in which boys and girls were taken to observe the rites of passage. Usually, after the rites are completed, the community of storytellers took over as educators on issues of ethics, religion, morality, and other social contracts.

Sometimes in order to reconcile with others, one must first reconcile with the self. Achebe (1994) again offers an example of someone reconciling with the self:

> Worthy men are no more," Okwonko sighed as he remembered those days. AIsike will never forget how we slaughtered them in the war. We killed twelve of their men and they killed only two of ours. Before the end of the fourth market week they were suing for peace. Those were days when men were men (p.200).

I shall now turn to a very important aspect of the process, and that is the narrative, the most essential element of the model. Under this subtopic, we shall look at narration a creative art form that has an immense influence on the process of mediation.

The Narrative Process in Mediation

If storytelling is the unfolding, the narrative is the technique of unfolding. It is interesting to note that many disinterested people attending mediation and negotiation processes in Africa, do so not to hear stories that they had heard countless times before. To hear the narratives of such stories is comparable to church congregants who, listening to sermons, do not go to hear biblical stories for the first time, but the narratives. Narrative is the political element in storytelling. In summarizing Freeman (2003) in a keynote speaker's address, organizers of a conference said "The self created in process of narrating is thus to be regarded not as some substantial thing but as a series of continuous tellings and re-tellings, issuing from the work of the narrative imagination" (p.1). Through the following example, let me illustrate the aspect of the continuous in order to illustrate the omnipresence of the narrative technique:

SCENARIO

Narrator: I decided on a particular Friday to visit the farm in question after my son could not get the other party to stop farming the land. (Then a continuation into the remote past) This farm was like a sacred place in the days of my grandfather, who everyone in the surrounding village knew was farming the land. I surveyed the land from a distance and realized that the boundaries that my father erected on the borders of the land had gone. My father had demarcated our land (myth making) on the orders of my dead grandfather. That was what my father told me. When I inherited the farm, I paid off all the debts owed by my father. I have since decided that I should (projecting the conflict base) divide the land among my three sons. But what did I see? (blame) There was Dauda with his children from across the stream, outside my village, claiming the land.

This kind of narrative expresses the omnipresence of more than just the conflict party. One of the conflicting parties is negotiating the past, the present, and the future so that the political base of this example can be appealing to the sentiment of the mediators who must see the need to keep a family unit intact.

The mediators are expected to visualize a construct that is larger than the conflicting parties and understand that this matter has the blessings of the dead, the living, and the unborn.

Counter-Scenario

I had asked my sons to accompany me to the piece of land on the Friday in question. I live just across the stream, but I certainly did not belong to a different village (legitimacy). My grandfather had been doing business with Sheku's grandfather for a long while before they both passed over to the land of the beyond. Before they both died, my grandfather had paid for the land that was originally owned by Sheku's grandfather. (Continuation into the remote past) My father had farmed the land countless seasons without anyone ever raising a finger against him. My father, who inherited this land, passed it over to me before he died many moons ago. (Continuation into the future) I had taken my children to the farm because they were off to the city, and I wanted them to know about all the assets that I have in the event that I died before their return.

The speaker of the counter-scenario wants the mediators to see that the claim of the speaker of the scenario goes outside a respected settlement. A strong political reference could be found in the speaker's mention of the wishes of the dead and the unborn.

Both stories are a narration of political apology. Parties take their turns telling their stories. In Africa, this opportunity can follow with an arrangement for parties to use every available means to tell their stories. We shall now look at the various arrangements parties make to articulate their complaints in mediation programs.

Arranging a Narrative Package

Obviously, the traditional African mediation ceremony is not the same as that of the West. In establishing a sitting for mediation, the mediators, who are mostly experienced officials attached to chiefdom courts perform the opening ceremony.

Through chants and sacrifices (usually, it is the blood of a lamb), they seek the intervention of the gods. The following (Joseph, 2001) is an example of a song from Malawai that in preparation for mediation is sung to the god, Ruwa, of the nation:

> We know you Ruwa, Chief Preserver.
> He who united the bush and the plain.
> You, Ruwa, Chief, the elephant indeed,

> He who burst forth men that they livedY
> Chief, receive this bull of your name,
> Heal him to whom you gave it and his children
> *(p.336-337).*

At the completion of the song, offers are made to the ancestors who have gone to the great beyond. The ancestors receive the slaughtered meat, a share of the wine of unification, and other food items. The mediators then turn to the living, and, beginning with the political and spiritual leaders, down to the ordinary well-wishers, they admonish the community to support the process. They ask for the blessings of the elders and the moral support of every member of the community. The opening ceremony could take as long as an hour, depending on the significance of the conflict, and the social standing of the parties. Maiese (2005) quoted Julius Osamba, who describes the East African experience as,

> The meeting would be held in a Acarnival@ atmosphere, punctuated with stories, songs, dance, proverbs, etc. The name of God and spirits would be invoked during the meeting. A bull would be slaughtered and its blood collected and sprinkled into the air as a way of binding the community to the peace covenant. As a gesture of reconciliation the whole group would eat the meat together. Thereafter, feasting, singing, dancing and

> celebration would continue for several days. The whole society would thus be part of the agreement and anybody who violated it could suffer some calamity (p.4).

The institution of African conflict resolution is traditionally a pageantry of events. A daiquiri of arrangements is put in place to heighten every angle of the procedure. Dancing and music underscore the narrative process. However, I must quickly mention that the music and dancing do not necessarily mean that the occasion is joyous. As well as moments of joy, there are moments of sorrow also; therefore, to express those different moments, participants intersperse their narratives with drumming.

Songs and Dance in the Narrative Process

Songs have always played a very important part in the socio-cultural development of Africa. In the mediation process, songs are important in the body politic of the narrative. The main mediating parties have their choral groups on the side; however, the groups only gain prominence when their mediating parties heighten a tune. Automatically, the choral group goes into action. Augsburger (1992) calls this kind of arrangement Athe eternal triangle in which there are the two parties and the issues; then the first ally is drawn in; then the other party's ally becomes involved. By now there are a number of triangles, and the number rapidly increases as the conflict circle expands. (p.152).

Usually, it is easy to tell when a song signifies happiness and joy or when it signifies sorrow or pain. Normally, joyous moods are expressed through fast music and painful moods through slow music. Additionally, it is important to note that music could be fast, but it is solely intended to help the mediating party explain how quickly an incident took place. Slow music could also mean that during an incident either the speaker or the other party was not showing interest in whatever was going on.

Let us examine some of the dances that a few ethnic communities use in their conflict resolution programs. This information is from Alkoli Traditional African Dances website as referenced below.

Adzohu: This dance originally functioned as a spiritual preparation for war, but today it is more a cultural or social event. Dancers wear colorful waist cloth, ankle raffia, bells and hats. The songs build self-respect and strengthen cultural identity in order to counter the influence of contact with the West. A vast repertoire of movements depicts battlefront cunning and bravery and among other things.

Agbekor: This dance is often performed at social/cultural events and at funerals. It is danced with horsetails and features spectacular slow and fast dance sections interspersed with many song interludes.

Anyako Atsia: This popular circle dance from the Ewes of Anyako features songs about morality, community, character, and pride.

Togo Atsia: A subtle and stylish women's dance from the Ewes of Togo. This event is traditionally organized by women and is used to present their point of view. Dance and music interludes are interwoven with short skits that focus on the challenges of modern life.

Other dances include *NanDom Bawa*, a Ghanaian dance of harvest celebration, *Gahu*, a Nigerian dance in which dancers wear expensive clothes and sing of being well-off and proud of it, *Tokoe*, a dance of girls coming of age into motherhood and requiring their independence, and *Gadzo*, a political and spiritual dance. In the category of songs and dance could be discussed with proverbs, chants, and poetry, all of which are used to produce similar effects.

Can the African Experience with the Narrative Mediation Model be Universal?

While the fact is not lost on me that African communities are collectivist in nature, I do believe that there are aspects of that continent's initiatives that can reform community well being and development in particularly non-indigenous societies like the capitalist West. I want to return to Winslade and Monk's book on narrative mediation. Although I have meticulously explained the traditional practices of narrative mediation in Africa, I think Winslade and monk have produced the Western version of the model articulately. I have no doubt that mediators will find it useful in mediating personal and community conflicts. It is not surprising that Australia led the Western world in the discovery of the narrative mediation model with the presence of the Australian aboriginals, whose culture is as high context as those of Africa.

Given the industrial challenges in the West, which has crowded every space in the labor clock, there hardly would be any time left for the pageantry of traditions that I have discussed to be observed in a Western mediation center. In fact, it is equally true that not even in Africa are all the traditions observed in any one mediation process. However, one could argue that technology can help us bring back all the traditional practices to our mediation room.

I posit that not only would the African experience with the narrative mediation model be universal, but also it would render all other models as mere branches of its grand sensation. The process, which partly requires a communications networking as well as a gymnastic networking, can cater for a healthy conflict transformation and a therapeutic wholeness that includes body, mind, and social health.

I have written elsewhere that there is not a society any more in the world that is exclusively individualistic or exclusively collectivistic. In fact, communities that are obsessed with either context can be completely normal only if policy makers cultivate a bit of either cultural context for the welfare of their citizens. I can see the West benefiting a lot from the opportunities that narrative mediation model, as practiced in Africa, has to offer.

Conclusion

I have shown that the narrative mediation approach is probably as old as the continent of Africa itself but the model is new to the West. By virtue of its characteristic nature, the model could only have originated in a society whose culture use music, songs, dance, proverbs, and poetry in every spiritual sense.

References:

Achebe, Chinua. *Things Fall Apart*. Anchor Books, New York, 1994. Alokli West African Dance (2001), www.alokli.com/site/dances/dances.html (Retrieved February 27, 2006)

Augsburger, David W. Conflict *Mediation Across Cultures: Pathways & Patterns* Westminster John Knox Press, 1992.

Frazer, Robert. *West African Poetry: A Critical History*. Cambridge University Press, London, 1986.

Freeman, Fred. Narrative Matters. ww.stthomasu.ca/conf/narrative/index.htm (Retrieved February 27, 2006)

Hansen, Toran. "The Narrative Approach to Mediation" in Whose Story is it Anyway? An Interdisciplinary Approach to Postmodernism, Narrative, and Therapy. Reprinted from www.mediate.com (Retrieved February 27, 2006)

Joseph, George. AAfrican Literature@ in Understanding Contemporary Africa. (eds) April Gordon & Donald Gordon. Lynne Rienner Publishers, 2001.

Katz, Neil H., Lawyer, John W. Communication and Conflict Resolution Skills. Kendall/Hunt Publishing Company, 1992.

Karen, R. (2001). *The Forgiving Self: The Road from Resentment*. Doubleday, New York.

LeBaron, Michelle. "Mediation and Multicultural Reality." http://www.gmu.edu/academic/pcs/lebaron.htm (Retrieved March 1, 2006)

Maiese, Michlle. "Theories of knowledge in Beyond Intractability". (eds.) Guy Burgess & Heidi Burgess. Conflict Consortium, University of Colorado, Boulder: http://www.beyondintractability.org/m/knowledge_theories .jsp (Retrieved February 27, 2006)

Mazrui, Ali. Cultural Forces in World Politics. James Currey: Oxford, 1990.

Moore, C.W. *The Mediation Process: Practical Strategies for Resolving Conflicts*. (3rd.ed). San Francisco: Jossey-Bass, 2003.

Winslade J. & Monk, G. Narrative Mediation: A New Approach to Conflict Resolution: San Franscisco: Jossey-Bass, 2001,

Wright, Robert. Nonzero: The Logic of Human Destiny. Pantheon Books: New York, 2000.

CHAPTER 12

Reading the Political Resume of a Leader in Time of War

The tiger does not boast of its tigritude. –Wole Soyinka

As Sierra Leone braces itself for its first post-war presidential elections in 2007, I examine the presidency of Ahmed Tejan Kabbah, who, after nine years (two terms) as controller of state machinery, will step down from that position and strongly push his vice president forward to succeed him. Outside of his party and constituency, Vice President Solomon Berewa hardly has a mandate of national franchise; therefore, in order to launch himself, he has to stem forth from whatever foundation his boss has built. The feeling that Kabbah, fundamentally speaking, has ever been the controller of Sierra Leone's state machinery is certainly not generic among Sierra Leoneans. Even if a dichotomy cannot be negotiated between the president's supporters and his detractors regarding the latter assertion, we can all agree that the leadership that steered the nation the last nine years has been and still is a rather unique one, mostly stumbling along its way, rather than sailing through it. Perhaps, a clear thesis might be couched in the form of a question: would President Kabbah's leadership deficiency adversely affect the Sierra Leone Peoples Party (SLPP) in the upcoming presidential elections?

Kabbah, who owes his emergence to political leadership to the military junta of the National Provisional Ruling Council (NPRC) of Valentine Strasser, has such a backlog of treasonable criminal offenses with the Sierra Leone government that political observers would not even have thought of him as a possible choice to head a committee mandated to search for a presidential candidate on behalf of a formidable party as the SLPP, which was poised to break the chains of political impotency that the All People's Congress (APC), the erstwhile ruling party, had knotted around it in the last twenty something years. (The SLPP had lost political power to the APC shortly after it had inherited it from the colonial masters in the early 1960s.) Surprisingly, the head of a committee to locate presidential material for the SLPP was exactly what Kabbah became on the eve of political pluralism acceded to by the NPRC on the uncompromising demands of the civil society. Of what elements, then, is Kabbah made that he could come from an obscure background to assume the presidency of a troubled nation, which, by all accounts, needed a person of sterner stuff?

A lawyer by training, President Kabbah conducted his professional career mostly as a "silent" technocrat. When he was at home in Sierra Leone, he leaned heavily on government civil service employment, and when he was abroad, he was in the United Nations' employment. Kabbah was not the go-getter type of technocrat, and, therefore, hardly competed for political office. Every position he had held, moderate administrative positions as they were, had been served to him on a silver platter. In Shakespearean parlance, Kabbah has always had power thrust down his throat. A soft speaker and a dutiful page turner on any podium and keeping strictly to written speech, Kabbah is never as urgent as the occasions over which he presides. For instance, during the war, whether he was talking to Sierra Leoneans from exile in a place where the world was desperately fighting to return him to power, or whether he was celebrating his return to political power, Kabbah counted his words, hid his emotions, demystified his epithets, created no surprises, and presided over with the same lethargy a vulnerable system. Even before he became a president, Kabbah was never too sure whether his destiny was conducting under his own star or that of his wife, Patricia, a lawyer herself, who died some four years ago.

When finally Kabbah's name was paraded to fill the vacuum of SLPP leadership, references to his wife's southern background strongly helped market his image. Closely observing Kabbah in the years of the civil war, I noticed that his political deficiency became more apparent after the death of his wife. There is no doubt that while his wife was alive but ailing, many party stalwarts distanced themselves from his administration, but for the sake of the party, they remained silent about his blunders.

Among the party stalwarts with whom Kabbah struggled was his then vice president, Albert Joe Demby, who, like Kabbah, was a political loner. Demby, who is said to have financially bought himself a ticket to the vice presidency, saw Kabbah more like a party "outsider" who had only been privileged the presidential position in order to give several national identities to the party at a time it was being smeared with all kinds of ethnic accusation. Unfortunately, Kabbah had not quite achieved the national image for which he was elected. Demby, on the other hand, had been led by the party rightist into believing that he was the true-blooded DNA material for the party leadership and that he was more than a vice president—a president in waiting. Therefore, with Patricia Kabbah now dead, and the sentimental bridge between her husband and the rest of the party broken afterward, Demby had the right to request Kabbah's position.

After it became apparent that Kabbah was not the messiah for which Sierra Leoneans were yearning, questions regarding who Ahmed Tejan Kabbah really was began popping up. Until then, Kabbah's stint with the United Nation's had been enough to buy him the hearts of Sierra Leoneans. Before Kabbah, Sierra Leoneans had been used to having presidential material with more brawn than brain. With the United Nations behind him and a legal background in his resume', Kabbah was certainly going to map a fertile cause for the country. He was considered a new breed of politician, one who had no relationship with the failed leaders the country wanted to remember no more. The country perceived him as one whose history began from the time he came to Sierra Leone's political limelight from the UN, where it was widely believed, he had perfected the true art and science of bailing out failed states like Sierra Leone. To paraphrase Kenneth Kettle, who writes about the Nigerian writer, Cyprian Ekwensi, as quoted in Eustace Palmer's critical analysis of African novelists [1], if Kabbah was not repeating his political blunders, he was stumbling upon spectacular new ones. Thus failing the nation and disappointing every hopeful citizen, his detractors gathered the courage to revisit and rewrite the history of Ahmed Tejan Kabbah as he truly was.

A very disturbing past in Kabbah's professional career was a 1967 Commission of Inquiry set to investigate an alleged fraud at the nation's then only agricultural monitoring and producing body, the Sierra Leone Producing Marketing Board (SLPMB). The SLPMB, notorious for the corruption of its officials, suffered great financial losses and collapsed the nation's dream of food self-sufficiency at the time Kabbah was working there. Although Kabbah had escaped detention and gone abroad while the inquiry was being conducted, the commission continued to investigate him and later found him culpable of the charges. The government seized his houses and any other assets he had made for himself while he was in Sierra Leone. As part of President Kabbah's administration's campaign to distort this truth, Sierra Leoneans who dared to broach on the topic were pursued with treasonable vendetta. Paul Kamara, editor of *For Di People* newspaper and a fearless journalist, was sentenced to a four-year jail term for publishing the excerpts of the commission's report.

A Technocrat on Islamic Ticket

President Kabbah was born in Pendembu, Kailahun District, in the Eastern Province of Sierra Leone, on 16 February 1932. His family, educational, and religious backgrounds reflect the diversity and high level of tolerance that generally characterize the people of his West African homeland.

Born of Moslem parentage and a devout Moslem himself, President Kabbah received his secondary education at St. Edward's, the oldest Catholic secondary school in the country. President Kabbah also married a Catholic, the late Patricia Kabbah, *nee* Tucker, who hailed from the Southern Province.[2]

Up until Kabbah's arrival at the nation's political platform, an Islamic background was not a viable ticket to the Sierra Leone presidency. The farthest any Sierra Leonean with an Islamic background had gone was the vice presidency. That record was established by Sorie I. Koroma of the APC under the presidency of Siaka Stevens, who was followed by A.B. Kamara of the same party under the presidency of Joseph Saidu Momoh. Despite a current statistics that shows Muslim 60% indigenous beliefs 30% and Christians 10%,[3] a statistics that to a large extent echoes previous ones, the political reality is that while Sierra Leoneans who maintain an Islamic faith are in the majority in the country, the mantle of leadership is largely in the circle of Sierra Leoneans who maintain a Christian faith. While Kabbah's political emergence is a religious shuttle in the Christian crypt, his Islamic orientation is not likely to matter when he vacates power. The current leadership of the APC and the SLPP are Christian dominated.

Does religion play a major role in the politics of Sierra Leone? Certainly, the arrival of an Islamic president in the person of Kabbah in 1996 bought Sierra Leone a new round of excited friends from Libya, Iran, Egypt, and Nigeria, (the latter a multi-religious state with a strong Moslem leadership headed by Sani Abacha, which practically saved the presidency of Kabbah.)

Politics in Sierra Leone since independence has tended to

be Anglo-Saxon in nature, rooting much of its tradition from Britain's Downing Street tradition. We need not be reminded that Sierra Leone was colonized by the British. Before that and beginning with slavery, the two countries have shared many intellectual and cultural values. Even with Islam consuming 60% of the population and Christianity just 10%, the social institutions in the country overwhelmingly have a Western Christian outlook. This kind of political contract has its roots in what Mazrui (1990) considers "a fusion of religion with sovereignty in this treaty as the religion of the prince was deemed to be the religion of the principality, the king's faith was the faith of the kingdom" (p.19)[4] Mazrui further points out that in such a contract, (p.19) "the decision to equate the religion of the king with the religion of the kingdom was a principle of no interference in the different princes' internal religious affairs."[5] This statement was especially true of the APC presidency in the 1970s and 1980s. Islam maintained the cultural power while Christianity maintained the political power. At the center of this arrangement was the not-so hierarchically organized indigenous religion, which at one time was very popular because politically minded Moslems and Christians alike consulted it to conjure themselves to political leadership.

Although Sierra Leoneans generally tend to look upon themselves as religiously tolerant, the reality is that the official face of Sierra Leone has continued to be predominantly Christian. While the circumstances surrounding Kabbah's presidency cannot be primarily explained in the context of Islam, it must be noted that Islam played a subtle role in Kabbah's prominence in the 1996 elections. After Kabbah had dutifully served the military government of the NPRC, the SLPP, which by then had established a very good relationship with the junta, inherited the lawyer from the junta for its future struggle. However, Kabbah was not a prince in the eyes of the SLPP; instead, he was more like a consultant on whom the SLPP banked to save the party from any legal mess in the event that the constitution finds it wanton. About this time, the SLPP was then a little relaxed on its fear of an APC comeback because most of that party's henchmen were either in junta lockup or in exile.

Later as the pressure on the military junta piled up to vacate power, the need for party consolidation became a necessity. If the junta were going to be chased out of power, it certainly could fuse into one of the political parties: the SLPP came in handy. For a starter, SLPP and the NPRC had a mutual friend in Kabbah. Although Kabbah still had the SLPMB stigma in his historical cupboard, not many people were aware of it. All that anyone knew about him then was that he had helped the NPRC drafted the nation's constitution, which was a big achievement for a nation that felt cheated by its leaders. Again, it should be clear as to why Kabbah's criminal past did not automatically surface —he had never had a political struggle for office, or any cutting-edge past anyone can remember. Even at the international level, the name of Ahmed Kabbah never racked up any memory of political or leadership envy compared to John Karefa-Smart and Abass Bundu, international figures of worth, and members of other political parties, who put them up against the presidential bid of Kabbah in the 1996 elections.

Quick-fixing Kabbah

John Karefa-Smart, an octogenarian politician, is said to have been the man whose obstinacy opened the door of political leadership for Ahmed Kabbah. Given that Karefa-Smart, who had served almost every government in Sierra Leone since independence, and who, was attached to the founding of the SLPP, was tapped for the leadership after the SLPP realized that if it did not need to move beyond its ethnic and geographical quarters in order to attract to its top leadership people of other groups by every stretch, the race might not be in their favor. The last nightmare the SLPP was going to experience again was APC's return to power. The SLPP had almost crumbled into oblivion in the twenty something year reign of the APC. It had seen its many strong members prostituted for political office. The few hardliners the APC did not crack suffered under the weight of its power.

Nevertheless, an argument may be made that the SLPP was then paying the prize of its own evil intentions. Under the leadership of Albert Margai, for instance, the party indulged in a politics of territorial bifurcation. Although the spirit of nationalism had indiscriminately brought under the wings of the party "patriots" from every ethnic group, very soon, the southeasterners began laying the strongest claim to the party, and with Albert Margai pushing the country to a single party system, politics became polarized forever!

Although Albert Margai showed a stronger political leadership than did his brother, Milton Margai, whom he succeeded, Albert, sowed the gelatinous seeds of political infertility that dictators like Siaka Stevens sailed on throughout his tumultuous leadership. Therefore, by 1967, the SLPP was no longer a truly national political party. It had become a party of the Mende ethnic group. By this time, the northerners and their political leaders were struggling to identify themselves with a party of their own. They had been late to wake up to the reality that the SLPP, a party born in the north, was already the sole property of the southeasterners and their political leaders. When the krios and the northerners founded the APC, rumor has it that many of those present urged Siaka Stevens and other important figures to name the party SLAPC, meaning Sierra Leone All People's Congress, as long as it competed with the SLPP in order to have a national outlook in name even if not in character.

By then, the political drama was very tense with the British colonialists edging out of the country's economic arena they still wanted to be in. However, the Krios and some northerners had successfully undermined the British, the British, in turn, plotted against every one of their detractors who thought of inheriting their position. The contest eventually cleared a path for the SLPP, which by now was an entrenched southeastern political voice. Milton Margai was later called to Britain to walk on a red carpet. He returned home with the blessings of the queen to take the reigns of power from the British. The silver platter power the British handed to Milton Margai did not wait long to reveal its ugly face, and as Gordon writes,

The transfer of power to African decisionmakers was expected to end political repression and allow the perceived wealth of the former colony, siphoned off to Europe, to bring quick relief and instant economic progress to African professionals, businesspeople, artisans, and the huge ranks of the poor.[6]

Perhaps the SLPP was too excited about the leadership of the country to foresee the risks involved in receiving power from a colonial master who still had an eye on the riches in the colony. The British left behind what Gordon calls landlocked geographical units. The SLPP had the duty of introducing true democracy to a colony that never knew democracy under the British, and these "were essentially alien structures hastily superimposed over the deeply ingrained political legacies of imperial rule."[7] The northern and Krio political detractors did not make it any easier for the SLPP. Legend has it that the northerners were surreptitiously slaughtering domestic animals, creating every possible horrible sight in public places, and blaming the act on the SLPP's desire to sacrifice human flesh for political answers to the country's mounting problems. The SLPP was torn between the proverbial rock and hard place. The British continued to scavenge for resources and for the promotion of their culture. I have written elsewhere that

Sir Milton Margai, Sierra Leone's first Prime Minister, and a rural man who inherited the British legacy, had only to think British and act British. Any attempt by Margai to modify the game, in consideration of our values, would have shattered the foundation of his political authority.[8]

When finally the northerners, with the support of the Krios, had succeeded in forming a formidable opposition in the name of the APC, they sabotaged the developmental programs of the SLPP by convincing the voters to look upon the draconian rule of the SLPP as imperial as that of the British. Many had not forgotten how they suffered under the British. Therefore, in the 1967 elections, the APC swept the mandate, and for the next twenty something years, the SLPP was rendered only unconsciously alive, surviving on the feeding tube of the APC.

Government in the Tiger Jungle

During the war, no one had the privilege of knowing what the Kabbah administration policy was on anything. It did not matter how lengthy or how long radio programs were in the country, never was anyone going to hear any of the position taken by the Kabbah administration regarding the war, security, the economy, the unruly military, the uncontrolled militia, and the deadly conflict because there was nothing the SLPP government could offer the people of Sierra Leone. As it was, the Kabbah administration had its ears to the international radios, waiting to know what the UN Security Council, the, Economic Community of West African States (ECOWAS), the British Government, or the U.S. Government had decided about Sierra Leone. The news afterward, instantly reached Sierra Leoneans via international radios. It was only then that the government radio, with its anachronistic rendition of the national anthem, cleared the path for the president to inform the nation what was going to happen in Sierra Leone. The SLPP government had become a laughingstock. Didn't Mazrui remind us that "…those who capture the state will discover that they are captured by it"?[9]

Even among his friends, hardly anyone has shown enthusiasm for President Kabbah's administration. The problem these friends and indeed most citizens have with Kabbah is not so much about what he didn't achieve, but what he didn't do right. With his most recent detractor, Emanuel Grant, a former ally and Minister of Energy and Power who dared to paint a very poor image of both President Kabbah and the SLPP, the list of cronies who have vacated the president continues to pile. Among them is James Jonah, who had been Kabbah's ally since their days in the UN. He had rallied to Kabbah's call when the prospect of the latter became apparent that he was going to run as candidate for the SLPP. It would not be a surprise that Jonah might have been talked into accepting the leadership of the electioneering wheel by their boss, UN Secretary General, Kofi Annan, who remains the only friend not to abandon Kabbah, even when it is apparent to him that Kabbah is a failed president. As for Jonah, he threw off the unbearable gauntlet of the Kabbah incompetence and bade Kabbah and his administration goodbye.

It is important to turn back the wheel of time to see what a few other people think of Kabbah. Ghana, the second most West African ally of Kabbah during the Sierra Leone civil conflict, poured not only a lot of money, human, and technical resources to ensure stability for Kabbah's administration but also from time to time Ghanaian President Jerry Rawlings dispatched his officials to visit Sierra Leone to help Kabbah with policy matters regarding the prosecution of the war. Fed-up with the ineptitude of President Kabbah, the Ghanaian leader at some point let the world to know, via the BBC, that he didn't think highly of Kabbah and his administration. This statement came at the height of a military blunder caused by Chief Hinga Norman, who was the deputy minister of defense and who doubles as the head of the kamajor militia.

Norman's divided attention led to a broken national army. Kabbah, who was the Grand Chief Commander of the military forces, stood by as Norman made it difficult for the military to prosecute the war. Ghanaian soldiers, like their Nigerian counterparts, became trapped in the quagmire in which a national army had become second fiddle to a local militia. Norman's greed and military blunders greatly affected Kabbah, who did not know how to address the situation. The Ghanaian leader was greatly disturbed by the indiscriminate killings of his soldiers; he drastically reduced the number of his soldiers in Sierra Leone and redefined the presence of those left there in non-combative positions.

Perhaps the most troubling desertion was that of Charles Margai, a formerly important voice in the SLPP and the son of the party's former leader, Albert Margai. Although Charles Margai's breakaway from the SLPP does not in any way increase his chances of clinching the presidency of Sierra Leone in 2007, it will significantly sink the national promise of a rather hopeful incumbent. The circumstances that led Margai and Ambassador John Leigh, the latter (who later made amends with the party) a less threatening, but vocal SLPP member, to break away were blown out of proportion. The failure of the leadership of the SLPP to frustrate Margai from pursuing his plans of establishing his own political party showed the level of decay that had eaten into the fabric of the party. No sooner had Margai established his party, than members began slipping off the SLPP to join him. It is not only embarrassing to see a party in power losing its members to a new party, but also this desertion underscores that Kabbah is heading a disgruntled bunch of people, many of who are not only leaving the party but also would turn around and talk about the seismic future of the SLPP.

Kabbah's International Camera and the Promise of Political security

In running his government, Kabbah exhibits the hopefulness of V. S. Naipaul's fictional character, Mahesh in *A Bend in the River*. Like Mahesh, Kabbah is a photographer, committed to turning his political camera to the West, where he continues to look for workable policies as well as money to run his government. Naipaul's description of Mahesh is apt for Kabbah:

> The cameras were one of Mahesh's ideas that had gone wrong. Mahesh was like that, always looking for the good business idea, and full of little ideas he quickly gave up. He had thought that the tourist trade was about to start again, with our town being the base for the game parks… But the tourist trade existed only in the posters printed in Europe…[10]

In reality, the camera has been a valuable instrument not only for development but also for conflict control. Kabbah has never relied on his "little ideas:" instead, he gave up quickly on those in favor of the "touristic" ones from Europe. The danger was that whenever he wanted them to be real, they failed him. Europe and the outside world were never actually interested in what Kabbah wanted. They cared only about what they saw as a necessary promoter of their own agenda. Kabbah has always told Sierra Leoneans how much he relied on his international friends to help him help Sierra Leone develop. Kabbah doesn't seem to know that international friends must not always be brought to the same room at the same time. While Kabbah had the right to choose his friends, he certainly also has the responsibilities to be not only discreet but also discerning. For instance, Kabbah's continued association with Libya's Gaddafi has raised a few eyebrows in the West. Whatever the size and economic deficiency of Sierra Leone, its diamonds buried underneath are notorious for being bloody and supportive of Islamic fundamental terrorism. The West thinks of Sierra Leone as a soft spot for terrorism because of its diamonds. Paradoxically speaking, because of our country's chronic persistent poverty, and the leaders' insatiable greed and corrupt tendencies, our diamonds are considered nuclear weapons of mass destruction. By 2001, the West began believing that Al Jazeera and Hezbollah had infested Sierra Leone with their terrorist tendencies. Hezbollah actually does have a following in Sierra Leone. The following paragraph appears in the *Middle East Intelligence Bulletin:*

The fact that most Lebanese merchants have close family and business connections in Syrian-occupied Lebanon makes them extremely vulnerable to Hezbollah threats. "There's a lot of social pressure and extortionate pressure brought to bear: 'You had better support our cause, or we'll visit your people back home,'" explains Larry Andre, the deputy chief of mission for the US Embassy in Sierra Leone. "They're asking for contributions . . . Will they use threats? Sure," says Joseph Melrose, one of Andre's predecessors. Because so much of the trade is illegal, victims of Hezbollah extortion are reluctant to seek protection from the authorities.

A glimpse into the scale of Hezbollah profits from the diamond trade came in December 2003, when a Union des

Transports Africains (UTA) airliner loaded with Lebanese passengers crashed off the coast of Benin - on board, according to news reports and Western diplomats in Sierra Leone, was a Hezbollah courier carrying $2 million.

Whereas Hezbollah derives revenue in Sierra Leone primarily through extortion of Lebanese merchants, in the Congo, which has been wracked by civil war since 1998, Hezbollah operatives "muscled their way into the business" and began purchasing diamonds directly from miners and local middlemen at a fraction of their market value. The highest quality stones are sold in the Belgian diamond marketing hub of Antwerp, while the bulk are sold in emerging diamond markets where the organization can operate more freely, such as Bombay and Dubai.[11]

How does the president of a neutral country convince its many international friends that the Sierra Leone government does not support or condone any terrorist behavior? While the Lebanese prate about their citizenry in Sierra Leone, they are forever tied to the biological concerns of Lebanon. Therefore, they have become a threat to Sierra Leone's development. When an immigrant force, like the Lebanese who maintain the jingoistic patriotism of the first home country, controls the economy of the second home country, the interest of the second home country is only as important as long as it can be milked to support the interest of the first home country. The biggest weapons these Sierra Leonean-Lebanese use to fund the various fighters in Lebanon are the Sierra Leone diamonds. A diamond rich neutralist country like Sierra Leone can easily find itself in international terrorism mix-up after the events of September 11, 2001.

Conclusion

After five years of absence from Sierra Leone, I returned to conduct a writer's workshop in July of 2006 and did not help noticing that the provision of electrical power had become the individual private enterprise of the citizens. There were two large corporations the people could turn to: The duty was divided between two leaders. By day, God provided the electricity of sunlight, and by night, small Honda generators from Asia, with a brand name known as "Tiger" with unbearable noise pollution, provided light for them. My suspicion is that someone who wanted to associate generator pollution and other regularly occurring fatal accidents to a national breakdown and state failure, found a way of linking the problem to the leadership crisis of the Kabbah government. An appropriate antithetical name chosen to ridicule the lackluster Kabbah administration was Kabbah Tiger!

References

[1] Palmer, E. An Introduction to the African novel, Toronto, Heinemann Educational Books Ltd., 1972
[2] http://www.statehouse-sl.org/biodata.html (retrieved March 13, 2006)
[3] http://cia.gov/cia/publications/factbook/geos/sl.html?CFID=5224&CFTOKEN=30805490#People (retrieved March 13, 2006)
[4] Mazrui, A. (1990). *Cultural Forces in World Politics*. Oxford:James Curry, p.19.
[5] Ibid, p.19.
[6] Gordon, D. L. (2001). "African Politics" in *Understanding Contemporary Africa*. (eds) April A. Gordon & Donald L. Gordon. Boulder: Lynne Rienner Publishers, p.56.
[7] Ibid, p.60
[8] Hallowell, G. (2005). *Tears of the Sweet Peninsula: May 25, 1997 and the Sierra Leone Civil Conflict*. Baltimore: Publish America, p.28.
[9] Mazrui, A. (1990). *Cultural Forces in World Politics*. Oxford: James Curry, p.57.
[10] Naipaul, V.S. *A Bend in the River*. New York: Vintage Books, p.51.
[11] "Hezbollah and the West African Diamond Trade" in *Middle East Intelligence Bulletin*, Vol. 6. No. 6-7, June-July, 2004.

PART III
ON THE MEDIA

CHAPTER 13

The Need to Improve the Media in West Africa

Because all of West Africa share common political and social challenges, it is possible, to a large extent, to generalize the operations of the West African media. For instance, Ghana and Nigeria of have provided many interregional training for a large number of West African journalists. Also, there is a growing cross-media employment network among West African media. At least two Nigerian-owned newspapers operate in Sierra Leone; a dozen Sierra Leonean journalists live and work in the Gambia; Ghanaian columnists contribute to the Nigerian and Sierra Leonean media; and several West African media pull their stories from all around West Africa. Although it is easy to determine that the media organization of one West African country is more advanced than another, the socio-political challenges facing the media in Guinea are not, for example, different from those inundating the Nigerian media.

In determining which media among television, radio, and print have the highest presence, it is easy to say the radio, since many more people all over West Africa, in urban as well as in rural communities, listen to the radio than read the newspaper or watch television. A large chunk of radio programs are not only orated in local languages, but also they are equally free to access. However, politically speaking, the print media not only have ubiquitous presence, but also the tendency to create a legacy of information of affairs as conducted especially by political leaders for posterity to judge and for the wider international community to peruse. So, in equal terms, the radio and the print media have the highest presences. The arrival of the Internet and its several uses as media outlet has added more challenges to the democratic and human rights processes in West Africa.

The West African media are therefore equally inundated with challenges. As political West Africa is transitioning from dictatorship to democracy, Journalists are expected to operate in an increasingly democratic and secured atmosphere, while exhibiting a high degree of professionalism in their reporting. But this picture is not always so rosy everywhere in West Africa. In many cases, if it is not the journalist abusing the profession, it is the authority abusing the journalist. As recently as in March 2009, the Media Foundation for West Africa (MFWA) met in Accra, Ghana, to discuss legal, national, and regional mechanisms they want to put in place to protect the media from political repression. The meeting established that many of the West African countries have repressive and unlawful legislation on media and freedom of expression. They are used by governments to silence journalists and citizens. Several journalists are jailed for defamation, false news, sedition, and offence against the head of state among others.

Open to this organization are the Community Court of Justice of the Economic Community of West African States (ECOWAS), and the newly established African Court of Justice and Human Rights based in Tanzania. True to MFWA's resolve, the organization has recently sued the Gambian Government in the ECOWAS court for the repression of the Gambian media, in what has been widely considered an unlawful jailing and torturing of Musa Saidykhan, a Gambian journalist in March of 2009 with The Independent, newspaper..

However, in addition to political repression, there are religious and cultural repressions as well, which are not usually given equal weights, but in many instances, can be more harmful to journalists, as in the case of Isioma Daniel, a Nigerian journalist in the This Day newspaper. 2002, Daniel dared to make a general comment about the prophet Mohamed, whom she said would probably have chosen a wife from among an expected group of beauty pageants for the first time contesting in Nigeria for the beauty of the universe award. Instantly, Nigeria was gripped by a religious anger as Moslems and Christians engaged in a fratricidal conflict.

Daniel herself later described events that followed her going into hiding.

When I browsed through the Google news site I read the fatwa by the Zamfara state government through their spokesperson, Mamuda Aliyu Shinkaf. "Like Salman Rushdie, the blood of Isioma Daniel can be shed. It is abiding on all Muslims wherever they are to consider the killing of the writer as a religious duty." I felt calm. It was then I realized that there was no going back to Nigeria. This situation was no longer a lie-low-until-it-all-blows-over-then-you-can-come-back scenario. Two hundred people dead in the name of religion.

A second abuse I noted is done by people in the media, whom much has been said about not always acting professionally, thus, not only endangering their own lives, but allowing others to cast aspersion on the profession of journalism. Wherever in West Africa, governments and ordinary citizens have continually complained that the media have been acting recklessly—flouting the ethics of the profession or not doing their homework well before disseminating news—and that in the process, decent people and institutions are regularly maligned. In many instances, the international media, such as the BBC, are considered more credible than are their West African counterparts.

It is important then that we say a word or two about human rights reporting in West Africa. There are several reasons for which it is important that the West African media increases and monitors human rights reporting. Among the reasons are that (1) most of West Africa is experiencing transitioning democracies; therefore, the media constantly need to be vigilant in reporting the processes of democratization, (2) and tied to that reality is the fact that much of West Africa depends on donor funding to be used for the common good. Are there issues of social justice both in terms of equity distribution and issues of corruption in the use of these funds and other national opportunities? Through a journalism of civic, political, and socio-economic rights, the media are able to document and evaluate human rights performance.

Given that in all of West Africa and even beyond, the process of becoming a media professional is very relaxed, both legally and professionally. There are, however, many a time when, at least, one in every three reporters needs extensive training in understanding content materials, human rights and responsibilities, and the ethics of the profession. Although there are growing numbers of media departments in West African universities, they do not usually provide the practical needs of practicing journalists, who sometimes don't have the requirements to enroll in such schools. At times, even the professors at these universities have not themselves first been practicing journalists, thus ensuring only a heavy dose of theoretic disciplinary schooling for those who go through these media schools, and who eventually aim for high paying UN and other attractive places.

The backbone of journalism is the reporter. In West Africa, many of those who become reporters are high school graduates or dropouts, with only the ability to construct "immediate" sentences here and there. It is these people that the bulk of the media training attracts. As investigative journalism has begun experiencing discourses in West Africa, because repressive governments and citizens accuse people in the media of not digging deep enough to be too sure of what they write about and because the reporters themselves complain about legally-impeded access to information, and about investigative reporting being expensive. The need for further and continuous on-the-ground training cannot be overemphasized.

References

Daniel, Isioma, "I Lit the Match" in *The Guardian*. Monday February 17, 2003.

Media Foundation for West Africa (MFWA)'s network of lawyers meets in Accra. March 31, 2009. http://www.mediafound.org/index.php?option=com_content&task=view&id=325 (retrieved September 2, 2009).

Press Statement: ECOWAS Court dismisses Gambian government objection. June 30, 2009.

http://www.mediafound.org/index.php?option=com_content&task=vie&id=325 (retrieved September 2, 2009).

CHAPTER 14

Addressing Human Rights in the Sierra Leone Media

A lecture delivered at the British Council, Freetown, Sierra Leone, and organized by the Institute of Public Administration and Management (IPAM), University of Sierra Leone, April 17, 2008

As Country Director of Journalists for Human Rights (JHR) Sierra Leone office, I find myself constantly defining and redefining my role on the landscape of Sierra Leone journalism and human rights. I cannot help maintaining a global view of my job and maintaining a global relationship with the media people with whom I work. I have many friends among owners and editors of electronic and print media houses. I engage them on the phone on a regular basis, admonishing one or the other to send participants to our monthly workshops facilitated by JHR's expert or to beef up their human rights coverage of national issues. My informal telephone conversations with many of these editors, radio station managers, and their reporters have at times warranted me to explain further the JHR concept and the relationship between journalism and human rights. My thesis for this lecture is that the media is experiencing a growing human rights and leadership crisis both within and without as a result of its sometimes monochromatic and sometimes unclear approach to issues of national development.

As far as some of my journalism colleagues are concerned, not only have they always covered stories on human rights, but also they have regularly created columns in their papers or radio programs on issues dealing with human rights. My job, like that of the expert and other trainers with whom I work is to dialogue with these journalists regarding JHR's concept of human rights journalism. In fact, one way of driving the JHR concept home is to explain that not only should journalists or reporters endeavor to write *every story* with a *human rights interest*, but also they should include the voices of the target group and other stakeholders in the story. In that way, it would be not only the journalist, sitting behind his or her mahogany table, theorizing on human rights.

I want to address a very unusual concern I feel is affecting the practices of journalism in Sierra Leone. To me, the issue of leadership in the media has become one of crucial concern. *Leadership in the media?* Yes, leadership in the media. In fact, I am actually saying that the Sierra Leone media is currently a victim of leadership crisis. It is my view that leadership has an element of human rights in it as much as human rights have an element of leadership in it. Leadership and human rights deal with insights, the value of being, and common dialogue, especially in a country like Sierra Leone where the culture, given to a dialogue of the deaf, has long existed in all facets of our interactions. JHR has voted the media the most effective vehicle for reaching a large number of people, all classes of people, and at all times with the comprehensive package of the culture of human rights. In this regard, JHR believes that a good understanding of human rights journalism is capable of making journalists and, for that matter, the entire fourth estate an effective partner in development. However, it has become worrisome to think that the Sierra Leone media, perhaps the best hope of disseminating and defending all tenets of human rights, has itself become a constant abuser of human rights.

As I posited earlier, the fourth estate is experiencing a leadership crisis. Among accusations levied against the media is its flagrant disrespect of the human rights of the public and citizenry. Similar pictures within the media have negatively touched on the leadership of an institution that should otherwise be, politically speaking, not only the third force but also the watch-dog of all.

I need to define quickly the kind of leadership that I talk about when I talk about the media. It is obvious that one cannot simply talk about the management of the Sierra Leone media in strict bureaucratic language, but one can talk about leadership of the media in a hegemonic sense. The media is arguably the world's largest institution in empiric terms even without sounding corporately hegemonic. You may want to ask about where all this rhetoric is leading me. The point I am trying to make here is that even with its gigantic structure, the media cannot be characterized as a conglomerate organ. While the media is not a clay giant, it does have the soft mind of a god. Victims and perpetrators turn to the media to defend and to confess their actions. We have been trying to niche a definition of leadership that we think should be associated with the media. First of all, we have carved out a place for the media in our day-to-day existence; and have shed any conglomerate thinking we may have about the media in our democracy. Now we are left to find a definition of leadership in the media. Perhaps any working definition of leadership in the media should take into account the concept of the protection of interest of human and idealistic expressions.

What are these human and idealistic expressions? We know these two to be packaged as freedom of speech; however, we know little about the elasticity of linguistic matter of which this phrase is made up. Article 19 of the Universal Declaration of Human Rights states that "Everyone has the right to freedom of opinion and expression; this right includes freedom to hold opinions without interference and to seek, receive and impart information and ideas through any media and regardless of frontiers." Let us decipher the rights in this article. Persons should be at liberty to nurse and hold any opinion and expression they so wish to hold and their rights to disseminate such opinions should be respected, enhanced, and protected. Often, in trying to align oneself with one aspect of free speech, bridled, unbridled, restrictive, unrestrictive, audacious or cultural, one journalist challenges the notion of another journalist, one media house stands up against another; and in the estimation of any of these parties, the other is always deliberately standing on the way of good journalism and good journalists. It would seem as if article 19 is encouraging individuals to stretch their private spaces indiscriminately, but that is not true.

Even a cursory reading through the length and breadth of the declaration will show one how responsibly one must conduct oneself. On a theoretic front, I want to bring in the principle of fairness, a concept that is at times coerced to fit the pocket of individual media houses. John Rawls (p.111-112, 1971), a thinker noted that, the principle of fairness holds that "a person is required to do his part as defined by the rules of an institution when two conditions are met: first, the institution is just (or fair), that is, it satisfies the two principles of justice; and second, one has voluntarily accepted the benefit of the arrangement or taken advantage of the opportunities it offers to further one's interests." It is normally good to view our individual and professional freedom of expression in the light of others' freedom and right to privacy—as we criss-cross the general lines of public spaces.

In the field of journalism, the potential for professional conflict increases as we seek to express or redefine the concept of freedom of speech. However, conflict in itself is as good a working tool as is breaking news. Courageous journalists always look forward to tension because it serves as an opportunity to exhibit character and professionalism. Ross Howard warns that "Professional journalists do not set out to reduce conflict. They seek to present accurate and impartial news. But it is often through good reporting that conflict is reduced." How does Howard's last sentence, that through good reporting conflict is reduced, sound to the ear of people who rendezvous with the Sierra Leone media on a daily basis? I will first of all do justice to Howard, whom all of us here should suspect, is referring to conflicts characterized by the news items journalists cover on a daily basis. Howard is helping to stretch a self-appreciation journalists have of themselves as security personnel of the nation-state; by way of extension Howard's mathematics of good reporting capable of reducing conflict does not sound true with the Sierra Leone media, in particular, the print media.

Viewed another way, we can say that if Howard is universally correct, then the Sierra Leone media is guilty of bad journalism. Real journalists do understand that conflicts have to be viewed from below their top layers. Howard has to be brought in here again with another quote, to show how journalism can serve this country in a more positive role. He writes: "By providing…information, journalism makes the public far more well-informed about the conflict beneath the violence, and can assist in resolving it." Mathematically speaking, Howard is envisaging a deeply isomorphic relationship transacting between the media and the general public, with the media needing only to demystify its impossible self in other to reconstruct an image of true partnership of development. The media should be at the helm of deliberative competencies. When it fails to see itself in that light, it takes away from society the ability to deliberate with itself.

We had earlier noted a phrase to take into account when defining leadership in the media: "protection of human and idealistic expressions." The Sierra Leone experience shows that between the media and the government, there has always been on the part of the media the accusation that government is strangling both freedom of speech and the throats of journalists. On the part of the government, the accusation is that the media is ringing both the neck of freedom of speech and that of the government. But the media, like the government, also has to present a picture of itself to the general populace other than what the government would have the populace think about it. Might we then think that leadership is or is not of real concern to the media? The question is what kind of leadership should the media provide? Increasingly, more and more proponents of leadership studies have viewed leadership as the art or science of influencing others to achieve a common goal. Because of the expression "influence," many management gurus have showed great warmth for this definition. People in the media are looking at leadership in a rather inclusive manner. The media does not seek to influence or educate others; instead, it seeks to inform others and to have others inform it. In the media, leadership is viewed as the ability to manage and disseminate information to enable consumers make informed judgments about themselves, others and their environments. That is the true character of the media. I should like to add that when people in the media go to press, they do so with the understanding that all media has gone to press. The business of informing others then therefore becomes a collect media act. At any one time that the process of managing and disseminating information happens, people in the media promise to protect each other simply by upholding the ethics of the profession. When those ethical tenets are in disarray, we can say that the media is in crisis. This lecture is necessitated by the critical mass at which the Sierra Leone media is operating now!

Like political parties, media houses in Sierra Leone seem to have their strongholds and weak holds. Perhaps a separate study needs to be conducted to determine how political parties in Sierra Leone for better or for worse, shape the media. There are possibly over a hundred independent electronic and print media houses in the country, and almost all of them are sympathetic to one political party or the other. Wherever the expressions "strongholds" and "weak holds" come from, they seem to have had the power to categorize not only the media but also many other institutions in Sierra Leone. After spending a little over five years in the United States, I returned to Sierra Leone April 2007 to assume the position of country director of JHR. I discovered that the two major political parties of the All Peoples Congress (APC) and the Sierra Leone Peoples Party (SLPP) could count on their several "friends" in the media. *And so what?* This kind of thing happens even in the United States.

Those who know the U.S. media will tell you which media house is sympathetic to which political party. Let us for the sake of time avoid any argument regarding the usual or the unusual practice of media houses sympathizing with political parties, move on to examining, among other matters the extent to which media houses have policed the interests of political parties. I have heard it said by Americans and immigrants alike in the US, that the CNN television network is sympathetic to the Democratic Party whiles their keen rival, the FOX television network is sympathetic to the Republicans. For over five years, every evening I returned from work, I have tuned to both television networks to get my news of current events in the US, that country's foreign policy, and other international news. In addition, I get the news coverage from other stations, regional and national. I can safely say to this august body that, while it may be true that there are media sympathies in America, for the most part, it is always difficult to determine which political party enjoys the sympathy of CNN or FOX. Either of these two media houses for instance, may be as liberal or as conservative as the Democratic Party or the Republican Party, but neither media house will mortgage their professional ethics over a conflict between the two parties. In Sierra Leone, the situation is quite the opposite. Evidence from the recently concluded presidential and parliamentary elections shows how media professionals tore each other all throughout the process to the extent that every radio program, every print issue had the metaphorical scavenging blood of the predator.

Can one talk about attitudinal change in the media? The government of President Koroma introduced a new culture, challenging Sierra Leoneans of all trades wherever they may be to seek to improve on their attitudes. While the challenge is a blanket one, the level and kind of change of attitude advocated is likely to be different in nature, structure, and character from group to group or from category to category, even within the same country. Unfortunately however, while the campaign has been well established, the government does not seem to have any theoretical basis upon which to conduct and influence the attitudinal change it so urgently desires Sierra Leoneans to improve on. That is just another matter. We have been used to having governments throwing challenges on us with no adequate guide, support, or clear vision. The call for attitudinal change is one such vague concept that no Sierra Leonean knows how to interpret, other than shouting it down one another's head, *u nor go change!* The Sierra Leone media is also baffled about what is needed to be done about attitudinal change, but as a matter of urgency and specificity, this paper will attempt to project what attitudinal change is needed within the media to enhance a journalism of development through unbiased reporting. In doing so, I will propose two theories to guide attitudinal change in the media. I have called the first one the Media Polity Theory and the second one the Meta-Communication Theory.

Without being too academically pretentious, I will define Media Polity Theory as the creation of media values through conferral authority. At the moment, the custodians of the profession seem to be SLAJ and other growing bodies—I am wary about including the Independent Media Commission (IMC) as a custodian body; however, not too long ago, the commission attempted to come up front with a series of media codes to help attitudinal change in the profession. The IMC codes however do not satisfy our isomorphic concerns regarding attitudinal change within the media. The IMC codes are appropriate under the Meta-Communication Theory. Under the Media Polity Theory, the media can develop frames and models. People in the profession are constructed and motivated by the enveloping frames. In practical terms, journalists and media houses should agree on an etiquette guiding their professional and personal conflicts. It must be noted that as part of personal and professional development, people in the media should learn how to agree to disagree at a superior level. While no single professional should define what attitude is valuable for the profession, the culture of the media should allocate actor-hood to media houses.

Let us talk about a recent publication that reconfigured the handsome Hollywood face of President Ernest Bai Koroma, giving him the Hellenic horns associated with the devil, while catapulting head-wards into the abyss of political disrepair. This lecturer was mesmerized by this new kind of journalism! I say new not in the pejorative sense but rather in the imaginative sense. Graphic journalism has not yet taken roots in Sierra Leone as it is in the West, where for instance, I have seen the many graffiti carved out of President Bush's face. I am not concerned about the dis-figuration of President Koroma, but in how that image has actually threatened to undermine the very virtue upon which Sierra Leone journalism is built. Perhaps it is more appropriate to say that the image should force us to look in the inside of the Sierra Leone media world and boldly deal with a few questions that have been rearing their heads even in the collective mind of consumers of media products. What has followed the caricature of President Koroma in the media has certainly been a product in bad taste to the consumer. Note that I have not said that the caricaturing of President Koroma was of bad taste or poor journalism. In fact, I have read in many of our local dailies, about descriptions of President Koroma that are more mentally disturbing than that of him with horns. However imagistic expressions have proved to be more urgent and compelling. Whether in defense of freedom of speech or in defense of some cultural taboo, the media like their consumers became divided over the matter of President Koroma's dis-figuration. In an atmosphere where journalists care so much about experimenting new experiences, Koroma's distorted image was an opportunity created for journalists to engage each other, albeit in a heated atmosphere to enable a deeper understanding of their trade while keeping their institution ethically intact. Instead, what we as consumers saw the couple of weeks that followed were media moguls "criminalizing" each other.

Following the publication, the owner of the newspaper was arrested or invited to the Criminal Investigation Department (CID). One writer paraphrased the president of SLAJ as saying that "the association has no stance in defending…on the recent caricature of the president...because she is not a registered member." Further down, the writer noted the SLAJ president as saying that the owner of the newspaper "should have a foretaste of the consequences of the libel laws" that she has supported all this while. He denounced the publication and called for the government's draconic media act to indict the owner of the paper. When I read that piece, I felt that the position articulated by the SLAJ president undermined the ideology upon which SLAJ and, indeed, journalism is built. I do not know how to separate the personal conflict between officials of SLAJ and the owner of the target newspaper from the conflict of interest that warranted SLAJ to assume such a stance on an issue that threatened to witness the abuse of one individual's freedom of speech. SLAJ may not have the moral duty to provide leadership to every Sierra Leonean journalist, but it does have the moral duty to provide leadership to Sierra Leonean journalism. SLAJ ought to view itself as a civil society organization that focuses on the ideology of free speech, a tenet that cannot and should not be compromised under whatever condition. For example, SLAJ could continue its conflict with the newspaper owner while condemning any intimidation on any member of the society for expressing his or her opinion, especially in the civil manner as was done by the target newspaper. But for some time now, leadership crisis has detracted the media from meeting with its obligation. Several media houses supported the position of SLAJ by criminalizing the owner of the target newspaper. The professional thing to do was to first chase the fox away, in this case, the government, and then turn around and rebuke the careless chicken, which is the owner of the target newspaper. When the media has a crisis and cannot maintain it at in-house level, society is starved and could not get the cognitive materials for attitudinal change.

I am happy to have suddenly discovered the term "criminalizing." As I continue to give examples of the crisis eating into the fabric of the national media, I will stick to the expression "criminalizing" for two reasons but only one deserves mentioning. Currently, the media is divided between accepting and rejecting the 1965 Public Order Act. According to detractors, the Act seeks to criminalize their professional shortcomings, in particular with regards to libel. Very often in their attempt to pass judgments on each other, individual journalists and national media houses have criminalized each other. At times even the consumers are condemned to turning leaves and leaves of pages of the print media over, only to have to read one castigation after another of one or other journalist, or newspaper, about how unprofessional, boot-licking, and shameless that journalist or paper has become. The news item does not seem to be any longer out there, but amongst journalists and media houses. National news reporting and highly needed analysis and assessment of issues in the media are almost becoming tentative taking back stage behind the constant quarreling of the media-might now perpetually sustained on front pages.

The old maxim *my learned colleague* associated with the legal profession significantly increases on the respect lawyers enjoy in Sierra Leone. Nobody says that lawyers don't have conflicts amongst themselves or that journalists should today begin to address themselves as learned colleagues as a way of reconstructing their public image. We will begin to appreciate good relationships amongst journalists and media houses when we see the civility with which they treat each other. It is worth mentioning here that as part of the Media Polity Theory, owners of media houses can eliminate a serious human rights abuse by upgrading the conditions of their reporters from people working for the remuneration of a mere byline to people working for appropriate financial benefits. In fact, proprietors and editors, by appropriately remunerating these sometimes over-labored reporters can help reduce or even eliminate the human rights abuse of extortion commonly referred to as *coasting*, the media is sometimes said to perpetrate against defenseless people.

The Meta-Communication Theory would be the collective ingredients that can be realized in any act of communication. Journalism is all about informing through communication. The media empowers citizens by informing them about the things happening within and without their environments. The purpose of informing the citizens is to enable them make informed judgments. To do so, the media should be careful not to taint their information. But every so often, the Sierra Leone media would try to be the complainant, judge, and jury. In January 2008, a paper had the following headline: "CONSPIRACY… CORRUPT OFFICIALS EXPOSED AT MINISTRY OF LANDS." With this headline, the paper has not only criminalized all officials at the Ministry of Lands, but also it has shifted the focus from the act of corruption to that of personnel incrimination. "CORRUPTION AT THE MINISTRY OF LANDS" will be a better front page cover, since the focus is directed at the un-condoned act of corruption. Names surfacing in the process of reporting cannot be said to have been criminalized. Whenever possible, the good reporter avoids adjectives and adverbs.

It is always advisable that a report on corruption should be a well crafted and engaging piece, describing the abuse-power of corruption. Usually, such news items allocate a few more paragraphs or sentences to the personnel involved if they already have a history of corruption. If they are new names, the reporter wants to concentrate on whether the corruption scandal has a history in the ministry or whether a network is involved. Are there external partners? Bear in mind that breaking news is only the beginning of a long journey into investigative journalism. Journalism of epithets as in the case of our above example is judgmental. The writer of the article under discussion did not set out to empower the public. The story ran from the front page to some inside ones, accusing a certain official of being corrupt. The reader was expecting more names as the headline promised. The news item was quite vague about the kind of conspiracy it had unearthed. Let us just say there was no conspiracy, and nobody was exposed; yet many people were abused!

In January 30th a newspaper had on its front page: "APC YOUTHS TURN SWEET BO BITTER WITH HARASSMENT." This story has a strong political undertone to it; therefore, any courageous and honest journalist writing such a story has to be in control of it from the start. The two major political parties of the APC and the SLPP having just concluded a national elections process that favored a winning for the APC and that at the same time cut short the political dominance of the SLPP could result into many power struggles. Against the backdrop that youths are vulnerable "tools" politicians can use to perpetrate, sabotage and destabilize communities, courageous journalists reporting stories of youth violence should engage all sides to the conflict but should refrain from editorializing their news items. The story in question is in bad taste, directionless, moving from the anger of one person to another, heightening the tension, indiscriminately tainting people in the public, and ironically speaking, tainting the reporter himself and the newspaper as well!

In the month of February this year, the gruesome and disturbing photographs of a beheaded woman, a suicidal victim, and that of a murdered business tycoon were published on the front pages of several newspapers. I have spoken to many journalists regarding the publishing of those pictures, challenging them to think of such photographic displays of the remains of private individuals as an act of abuse of their human rights. A few of these journalists think that visual information of the wicked acts done to Sierra Leoneans empowers the weak. However, must one mortgage the privacy of another to prove the wicked acts of certain Sierra Leoneans? "Featured is the remains of Marie Koroma, the six month pregnant woman who was last week murdered by her husband Musa Koroma..." one paper wrote on its front page; below the photograph of a prominent murdered victim. Another paper wrote about the dead "lying in a pool of blood," and three other papers also mounted the photo, identifying the victim by name. Perhaps the most horrible of all the photos was that of a man hanging from a rope. He was alleged to have committed suicide. The victim's complete identification, including his full name, his alias, even his residential address, was printed on the paper.

When I was growing up as a child in this country, I noticed a high level of respect and secrecy in the way my people dealt with the remains of their dead. Until a beloved dead relative was buried, the entire world of the living was brought to a standstill. The remains was mourned, bathed, treated, and clothed, with utmost care. Before the public was invited to pay its last respect, relatives placed the remains in a posture that would capture a compelling memory in the life and times of the now dead person. I am sure that my personal experience is generic. I loathe the day I wake up to be greeted by a published mangled photograph of someone I know. I think that the people, whose photographs are published in the papers I have talked about, belong to families, friends, and communities who were distressed by the horrible images. Remember that all along I have been talking about victims and the crimes that demised them. I think that for one to have died in a horrible manner, and to be paraded in like manner is a gross violation of one's right to privacy. It is my opinion that, to make for a compelling story, these reporters should have sought to find photographs of these individuals in their moments of integrity to accompany their stories. When readers behold those fine moments in their eyes, they weigh the stories very heavily in their hearts.

One other fair thing to do in a lecture like this is to also look at how vulnerable the Sierra Leone media has become to a point that powerful individuals and corporate Sierra Leone are abusing it at will on a daily basis. One disturbing culture in the media today is its over-dependence on press releases, conferences, and seminars for its main news items. As well, advertorial journalism now accounts for between sixty-five and seventy-five percent of newspaper and radio coverage. Against the backdrop of Sierra Leone being an aid economy advertorial and press release journalism, is suspect. In the West, media coverage is not so easily exploited by charity and non-governmental organizations nor does the corporate world easily summarize their corporate social responsibilities in podium jingles. Among the many secrets of the Sierra Leone media is that of the huge financial returns in granting space to corporate houses and non-governmental organizations. We are not talking about advertorial spaces; we are talking about advertorial journalism. Advertorial journalism is the understanding between the media house and the institution that coverage is not solicited, even though the coverage is highly paid for by the institution. This comes at the expense of "investigative" journalism. I use the phrase investigative journalism guardedly. All journalism should be investigative, and that's what I'm driving at. Much of Sierra Leone journalism has a dearth of investigation in it. Part of the reason can be attributed to the habit of media heads sending reporters to press conferences instead of sending them to search out news in the field. Because discrepancies can arise between press releases and actual happenings of events on the ground, investigation should be a foregone conclusion for any piece of news item.

While press release journalism has helped non-governmental organizations and corporations to easily articulate their positions and attract consumers, the media has not covered enough of their activities beyond those showcased in press releases and conferences. In their reporting, media houses have at times given us, word for word the contents of the releases as written and meant to be perceived by the reading/listening public. At other times, reporters summarize the releases, again, largely representing the views of the target organizations. In all of these arrangements, the reporter and media house practicing press release journalism could face with embarrassments if the press release representation is different from the reality on the ground. I would think that a good journalist would, armed with a release and encouraged by his or her media boss, follow up on several stories to the lead by visiting the field and engaging every stakeholder mentioned in the release.

The Sierra Leone media does not seem to have an articulated media philosophy around which individual journalists or reporters and media houses can be encouraged to develop their individual goals. A.J. Berry et al (1995) noted that "individuals have goals; organizations do not." What then can we say should organizations have if not goals? They should have positive ideologies that overtime can be looked upon as an organization's or an institution's culture of doing things. American journalists and media houses for instance are noted for having an ideology geared toward being the modern world media machine. Individuals wishing to be journalists and reporters in that nation must fashion their goals in line with the structural culture of the American media dream.

In the case of Sierra Leone, as the nation is bailing out of a decade long war, the media has the duty of mapping out both a leadership and purpose driven leadership. First, we must ensure that as a media we attract leadership that is prepared to step out of the traditional boxes of managing the media in ethnic arrangements, i.e. SLAJ for SLAJ, Reporters Network for Reporters Network, or women journalists for women journalists, in favor of a leadership characterized by ideological drive, even campaign. There are many of us here who believe that the Sierra Leone media has been at war with itself, and like the Phoenix burnt itself to ashes. To those pessimists or realists, Rhinesmith (1996) a leadership expert would say that with creative and imaginative leadership, the organization can emerge from that chaotic point of disorder with identified patterns, and that experience "can be used in understanding the larger transformation of systems even if their changes cannot be predicted in detail." And as Hersey & Blanchard (p.3) rightly states, "Many of our most critical problems are not in the world of things, but in the world of people." Therefore in bridging the realms of "things" and "people" to ensure effective change, there exists the need, to paraphrase Charles Joiner, Jr. (1987), for skilled leadership (characterized by creativity and imagination) (p.1) "that can integrate the soft human elements with (the) hard business actions" of the profession of journalism.

References

Media Foundation for West Africa (MFWA)'s network of lawyers meets in Accra. March 31, 2009

Hersey, P., & Blanchard, K. H. (1993). *Management of organizational behavior: utilizing human resources*. Prentice Hall: Englewood Cliffs.

Howard, Ross. *Conflict Sensitive Journalism: A Handbook:* International Media Support

Rawls, John. (1971). *A Theory of Justice*. Harvard University Press: Cambridge

CHAPTER 15

Sierra Leone and the Seismic Shift in the Media Landscape: A Situation Analysis of Information Power

> Address delivered at the Faculty of Social Sciences & Law Week, at the Mary Kingsley Auditorium, Fourah Bay College Campus, University of Sierra Leone, Monday September 05, 2016

> This paper attempts a social scientific approach to the seismic shift the media landscape in Sierra Leone experienced several years after the civil war, and, in line with the overall objective of the faculty week, it attempts to examine observations in order to construct a model of the new media platforms, and how information power, a little over fifty years since political independence, suddenly arrived at the hands of the ordinary consumer of media products. I use the interpretive model to understand the operations of this galaxy of media and their implications on peace and development in Sierra Leone.

> Keywords: Social media, media, information,

power, interpretive model

In the aftermath of the Sierra Leone civil war of 1991 to 2001, a seismic shift affected several developmental landscapes in the country. I argue that if war by itself is not a warranted and acceptable landscape, it usually enriches and embellishes other landscapes. Following the civil war, national developmental narratives and their behavioral demeanors were disoriented, seeking new breath; creative flavors catapulted from nowhere and invaded the comfort zones of citizens' dreary order, demanding citizens to surrender to redefined or new orders of behaviors. It is often believed that among major aftermaths of war is the unconventional emergence of creativity and imagination. In post-conflict societies, professionals and tradespeople of all categories, engage in enterprises that undertake to radically redefine or even re-institutionalize agencies of development and other social concerns in their communities.

This paper engages in interpretivist philosophy, and as the social scientist, Shutts (2006, p.43) put it, "believing that social reality is socially constructed and that the goal of social scientists is to understand what meanings people give to reality, not to determine how reality works apart from these interpretations." Interpretivistic approach in academia creates room for arguments, therefore, this paper agrees with Hart (1998, p.79) that "Being able to recognize the structure and substance of an argument is a necessary ability in everyday life but is especially so for the successful academic researcher." The paper, therefore, is tailored to the social design approach. Shutts pointed out the three basic principles of social design approach as being (1) Respect for persons i.e. "treating persons as autonomous agents and protecting those with diminished autonomy; (2) Beneficence i.e. "minimizing possible harms and maximizing benefits; and (3) Justice i.e. "distributing benefits and risks of research fairly." In keeping with this professional advice, I have conducted my observation with a generic eye, making no singular reference to any media organization in Sierra Leone.

A review of recent literature available on the media in Sierra Leone reveals that while the several analyses that exist, ran introspective views on the political state of the media, there remains no literature speaking to any seismic shift after the civil war. Yamba (2007) evaluated the media in Sierra Leone from their beginnings, following the establishment of the *Sierra Leone Gazzete*, in the eighteenth century, for instance, to their statuses in 2007. His analysis bordered mostly on the manipulation of the media by politicians, and the general financial starvation the media suffered throughout the period. Even after the civil war, as his paper advanced, Yamba did not make reference to any change in either the general perception of the media, by citizens, nor did he point to any growth in standards in the professionalism of the practitioners. If anything, Yamba noted, "The few trained, qualified and highly ethical journalists who refused to be corrupted by politicians [have] abandoned mainstream journalism, in favor of public relations jobs with numerous NGOs and the UN.

Press Reference is an online data input that sources from the media of various countries. It certainly has a lot of information on the Sierra Leone media, particularly useful to students of media studies. In addition to stating the history of the media, it discussed the unfavorable political and financial states of the media and the 1965 public order Act and its draconian effect on media practitioners. Of significance, it mentioned in passing, the establishment of a Mass Communication program at Fourah Bay College in 1993. However, it did not discuss the program or any other landmark event or concept as having impacted change in the profession. Oatley & Thapia (2012), through funds from Search for Common Ground, put together a more detailed introspection of the media in Sierra Leone. What made the work attractive to me was that it examined the media through the eyes of the youth, trapped in conflict. It was perhaps the only work, through empirical research, that dared to survey outside of mainstream media, to emerge with a statistical feel of the then growing influence of mobile phone media in the country. Their research found out that:

> Survey findings and statistics provided by the International Telecommunication Union (ITU) show that mobile telephone networks are the second-most-accessed media or communication device in Sierra Leone behind radio. From 2003 to 2008, the number of mobile phone subscribers in Sierra Leone grew nearly tenfold, according to ITU, growing from 113,000 mobile subscribers in 2003 to over 1,000,000 in 2008

In the 2008 Audiences capes household survey, around 40 percent of respondents said they had household access to a mobile phone. This percentage, while high compared to other estimates (ITU estimates 18.14 percent), hints at not only wider use beyond official statements but also the widespread habit of mobile phone sharing.

Let us accept these conservative findings for what they were. Obviously, it's been eight years since those findings. I have not been able to find any newer study. However, interpretively speaking, given the significant growth in the overall population, as reported in the just concluded Statistics Sierra Leone (SSL) national population census of 2016, and given that current demographics show that our population is more youthful in nature, it can be deduced that a significantly higher number of young people now have access to phones than it was the case in 2008. I must state here that whereas there are many articles online on the Sierra Leone media, hardly anyone surfaced as relevant to my paper, as Oatley & Thapia's "Media, Youth and Conflict Prevention in Sierra Leone." Although their paper did not tap too deeply into how the youth harnessed new media and technology, yet it began to lay the foundation for any researcher who might be interested to push further into studying media and technologies in Sierra Leone. Their conclusion on the matter noted that:

> The mobile phone network is transforming how information flows in the country. Journalists can now seek information from around the nation, expanding their coverage and accuracy without having to travel. This development applies to print, television and radio channels. Additionally, radio stations use mobile phones and SMS to solicit feedback and foster discussions with their listeners. It is now common practice for stations to open their phone lines at the end of discussion programmes for the audience to comment and ask questions. This process is opening up opportunities for greater citizen participation in governance issues.

Despite Sierra Leone being the earliest recipient of western media culture in the West African sub region, it picked up a slow pace of growth. There could be many reasons why this was so, yet only one deserves to be mentioned here. Unlike the other countries in the sub region, Sierra Leoneans, serving as guinea pigs, encountered the media at a time when the majority of its population was not only illiterate, but was far removed, as a capital consumer, from the satisfying products of the profession. At its inception, and going forward, the media merely served as a recording tool of the working machinery of the colonial government, and, particularly during colonial era, consumers of the media remained passive recipients of media products. To many natives living on the fringes of the city, the media was a rather elitist arrangement meant to gratify and to inform the governing elites of their own daily exploits. *The Sierra Leone Gazzete* could not be used to discuss any human interest stories, and therefore, those whose names appeared on its pages were either the white colonial masters, or those few African intelligentsias who possessed the white man's education, and had direct dealings with him.

At the turn of the century though, as mentioned by Oatley & Thapia, a certain European, known as Mr. Drake, came to Freetown and founded a newspaper called, *The New Era*, a rather ambitious project. From its seat in Freetown, the paper was meant to satisfy a readership of the entire holdings of the British colonial governments in the West African sub region. It therefore meant that intensely homegrown stories hardly made their way into the paper, unless they were of interest to readers in Ghana and Nigeria also, for instance.

Up until the civil war, only some of the print media managed to survive the draconian times, with only a few vehemently resisting any control or suppression by government. The print media continued to seem far removed from a good percentage of the population. For instance, papers hardly made their way to the provinces, where the population was denser. Even in Freetown, where the papers were printed, they remained the reading property of only the educated few, and one could further argue that, not all educated persons then, read the papers. Even though by the 1980s the media had become a powerful organ, its power was only limited to dissemination of information and not a solidifier of authority. The civil war came and went, and the media remained unchanged in every shape or form. Interestingly, however, while the media did not experience any change, because of its esoteric nature, it affected changes in several other landscapes.

By the mid-2000s, the catalyst that will forever change the outlook of the Sierra Leone media arrived in full scale, and it was called technology media. I had just returned from my studies in the United States, and I had still not been exposed to the new technologies that would touch the foundation of the Sierra Leone media. The seismic shift that occurred in the media not only destabilized the main stream media, but threatened to render its practitioners redundant. Amponsah argued that globally:

"…the most positive and productive surge

within the social media industry happened in the 2000s with the advent of platform such as Wikipedia in 2001, Friendster in 2002, Hi5 and MySpace in 2003, Flickr in 2004, YouTube and Reddit in 2005 and finally Facebook (publicly available) and Twitter in 2006. With the foundation firmly laid, other notable platforms such as WhatsApp in 2009, Instagram in 2010 and Snapchat in 2012 found success by appealing to audiences who were no strangers to sharing their information online."

By 2012, the focus of media power had shifted from the mainstream media to social media. Although there were social media such as Facebook, Linkedin, and Tanned, the technology that sent social media to its pinnacle was Whatsapp. In a short space, young people all over the country got connected to Whatsapp and became members of different Whatsapp groups. The Sierra Leone mainstream media were no longer the center of the information world. In fact, from the BBC to CNN and to local television and radio networks, all secured places in the social media. After a brief while, governments saw the need to follow after their citizens, by securing social media addresses and monikers, to share information, but what more to ensure that false information posted by detractors are easily corrected through counter information. From its inception, it was difficult for the government to control the social media or to regulate it. African governments didn't have the mechanism. The Western world which had created the media wanted to ensure unbridled access to every citizen of the earth to information, either manufactured by him or received by him.

Power and information are central phenomena to social media. The social media place information power in the hands of the consumer. However, unless the consumer acts responsibly, and treats information with the regards of maturity it deserves, anything and everything can go wrong. Many scholars believe that information power on its own is not enough if the consumer must continue to enjoy relevance in the media landscape. "Informational Power is the most transitory type of power," said one scholar, "Once you give your information away, you give your power away. For example, you share the secret, your power is gone. It's different from other forms of power because it's grounded in what you know about the content of a specific situation. Other forms of power are independent of the content."

Both Nye, Jr. (2008) and Slaughter (2009) underscored that power is connectedness. It is this connectedness Slaughter argued that determines who would be the "central player". She reminded us that all humans, and indeed all their activities are net-worked both at the vertical and the horizontal level. Society is networked; she argued that even unrelated activities are networked from vertical to horizontal, and that this reality affects the way power and power dynamics are viewed and exercised. Slaughter (2011) has also argued that power is at the vertical top, and that "the higher you climb, the more powerful you are" (p. 296).

I understand the focus of the faculty week to be looking at a situation analysis beginning 2018 to 2020. The year 2018 will pitch social media in the center of our presidential and parliamentary election. For better or worse, all eyes will be on the telephone screen and all fingers will be on the keyboards ready to dish out information, real or manufactured. Unlike the mainstream media, social media cannot be regulated, moderated or stopped; at least no one has, and should have the inclination to do so. Used properly, social media is perhaps the fastest vehicle to the path of development; used negatively, it could be the fastest vehicle to the path of destruction—and I dear say that I mean, for individuals and for nation states. And whereas there is immense information power in social media, there is no centrally identified leadership in its operations in Africa.

Most universities around the world are laying emphasis on social media studies and research. South Africa, for instance, comes out with an annual report on the state of social media in that country. It will be helpful if the faculty of Social Sciences, through the mobile phone companies, the National Telecommunication (NATCOM) and the Independent Media Commission (IMC), conduct frequent research to determine consumption of both technology and content. In that regard, the Faculty could further commit a few modules to the study of social media in relation to the development of the country and the technological growth of the citizens.

Government it seems is ahead of the University of Sierra Leone in that respect. In fact, it can be noted that most urgent press releases and public notices now appear on social media before they appear even on the national public broadcaster. And I think we all must understand the exigency of information to help both the producer and the consumer to respond quickly to situations. Having said that, it should be understand why government would regard social media with a suspicious eye. Just as there are hackers on the internet who have made their profession, the obliteration of every form of sanity, so are their social media users who would, and do have the power to distort any information on the domain, thereby create chaos and unrest. These are usually the kind of people whose actions offend governments and private people.

By now, all political players and observers are aware of the pivotal role social media plays and has to play in the coming 2018 presidential and parliamentary elections, and observers, such as the faculty and students of the Faculty of Social Sciences and Law, should begin to observe keenly if they have not already started doing so. Social media, if properly exploited can liberate people and their nation. In the absence of balanced social and cultural spheres of influence, where the political has remained the only powerful national institution, the social and cultural spheres are somehow subordinate. Therefore, it is important to note that the challenge of any government is to provide a leadership that fits the cultural make up of a given society, and part of that leadership should bring governments, institutions of learning, civil society organizations, and users of social media, to a common table, to be discussing the implications involved in harnessing the new media with seeming unbridled freedom!

I thank you for listening.

Reference

Amponsah, R. (2015). "The power of social media" The Market Mogul.
    http://themarketmogul.com/the-power-of- social-media/
Nye, Joseph, Jr. (2008). The powers to lead. Oxford University Press: 2008.
Oatley, N & Thapi, R. (2012). "Media, youth and conflict prevention in Sierra Leone" in Initiative For Peacebuilding: Early Warning.
    http://www.ifpew.eu/pdf/201204IfPEWMediaYouthConflictPrevention-Salone.pdf "Sierra Leone Press, Media, Tv, Radio, Newspapers" in Press Reference. http://www.pressreference.com/Sa-Sw/Sierra-Leone.html
    http://sourcesofinsight.com/
    information-is-the-most-transient-form-of-power/
Slaughter, A. (2009). America's edge: Power in the networked century. Foreign Affairs, Retrieved from
    http://elibrary.law.psu.edu/cgi/viewcontent.cgi?article=1014&context=jlia
Schutt, R. (2006). Investigating the social world: the process and practice of research, (5th ed.). Pine Forge Press: Thousand Oaks
Yamba, M.S. (2007). "The Media in Sierra Leone" in The Patriotic Vanguard.
    http://www.thepatrioticvanguard.com/the-media-in-sierra-leone

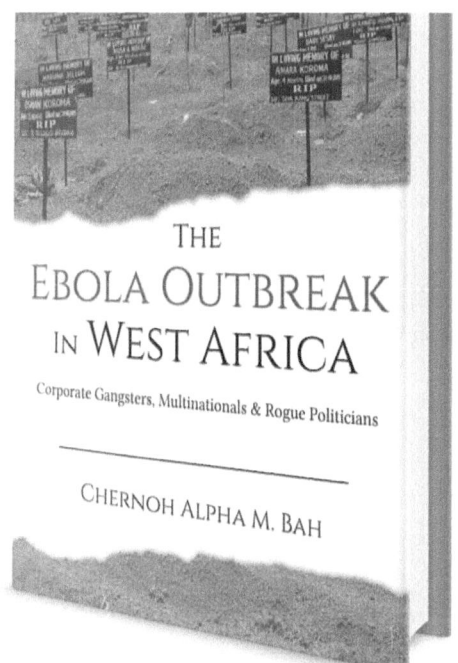

Also available from the Africanist Press:

The Ebola Outbreak in West Africa:
Corporate Gangsters, Multinationals & Rogue Politicians

ISBN: 978-099-697392-2 (paperback)
978-099-697391-5 (hardcover)

Publisher: Africanist Press
Author: Bah, Chernoh Alpha M.

Africanist Press books can be ordered through booksellers or by contacting
Africanist Press
Sales & Distribution Department
738 Washington Avenue (Apt 1A)
Brooklyn, NY 11238
+1 (347) 569-1978
africanistpress100@gmail.com

www.ingramcontent.com/pod-product-compliance
Lightning Source LLC
Chambersburg PA
CBHW030436010526
44118CB00011B/661